The Trail of Tears across Missouri

D0888214

Project Sponsors

Missouri Center for the Book

Western Historical Manuscript Collection, University of
    Missouri–Columbia

Consultant

Donald M. Lance

Special Thanks

Susanna Alexander

Marie Exler

Dorothy Merrill

Carol Morrow, Southeast Missouri State University

Beverly Baker Northup

Sharon Sanders, *Southeast Missourian*

A. E. Schroeder

Jewell Smith

Paul Szopa, Academic Support Center, University of
    Missouri–Columbia

Missouri State Library

State Historical Society of Missouri

Missouri Heritage Readers

General Editor,

REBECCA B. SCHROEDER

Each Missouri Heritage Reader explores a particular aspect of the state's rich cultural heritage. Focusing on people, places, historical events, and the details of daily life, these books illustrate the ways in which people from all parts of the world contributed to the development of the state and the region. The books incorporate documentary and oral history, folklore, and informal literature in a way that makes these resources accessible to all Missourians.

Intended primarily for adult new readers, these books will also be invaluable to readers of all ages interested in the cultural and social history of Missouri.

Books in the Series

Food in Missouri: A Cultural Stew,
by Madeline Matson

Jesse James and the Civil War in Missouri,
by Robert L. Dyer

On Shaky Ground: The New Madrid Earthquakes of 1811–1812,
by Norma Hayes Bagnall

Paris, Tightwad, and Peculiar: Missouri Place Names,
by Margot Ford McMillen

The Trail of Tears across Missouri,
by Joan Gilbert

The Trail
of Tears
across
Missouri

Joan Gilbert

University of Missouri Press
Columbia and London

Copyright © 1996 by
The Curators of the University of Missouri
University of Missouri Press, Columbia, Missouri 65201
Printed and bound in the United States of America
All rights reserved
9 8 7 6 5   07 06 05 04 03

Library of Congress Cataloging-in-Publication Data

Gilbert, Joan.
   The Trail of Tears across Missouri / Joan Gilbert.
     p.   cm. — (Missouri heritage readers series)
   Includes bibliographical references and index.
   ISBN 0-8262-1063-5 (pbk. : alk. paper)
   1. Trail of Tears, 1838. 2. Cherokee Indians—History—19th
century—Sources. 3. Cherokee Indians—Government rela-
tions. 4. Missouri—History—19th century—Sources. I. Title.
II. Series.
E99.C5G33   1996
973'.04975—dc20   96-10232
                                                            CIP

⊛™ This paper meets the requirements of the American
National Standard for Permanence of Paper for Printed Library
Materials, Z39.48, 1984.

Designer: Stephanie Foley
Typesetter: Connell-Zeko Type & Graphics
Printer and binder: Thomson-Shore, Inc.
Typeface: Palatino

To my mother, Blanche Sewell, and to the Indian women who
befriended her in Oklahoma many decades ago.

Memorize this tree
and the music of its leaves;
put your face against its bark
one final time. . . .
If you must have a keepsake,
pull a rose,
but keep your tears inside.
All have their own to hold.

—Joan Gilbert, "Cherokee Farewell"

Contents

Acknowledgments

Individuals of Cherokee heritage in North Carolina, Kentucky, Missouri, and Oklahoma have generously shared their knowledge and materials with the author during the writing of *The Trail of Tears across Missouri.* Cherokee agencies and museums, organizations commemorating the Trail of Tears, libraries, historical societies, and individuals interested in the history of the Cherokees have provided documents, information, and photographs.

Special thanks are due to many. Joan Greene of the Museum of the Cherokee Indian and Alan Smith of the Cherokee Historical Association in Cherokee, North Carolina, provided careful and detailed information and illustrations. Earl Stewart of Grayson, Kentucky, shared his writings and family materials. Virginia Brenner of the *Golconda (Ill.) Herald-Enterprise* and Darrel Dexter of the *Anna (Ill.) Gazette Democrat* sent both photographs and information regarding the 150th anniversary commemorations. Geneva Davie Wiggs of Wolf Lake, Illinois, told the story of Winstead and Anna Davie, who offered shelter to the Jesse Bushyhead family when they were stranded in southern Illinois by ice in the Mississippi River.

In Missouri, Marie Exler, historian of the Trail of Tears State Park area in Cape Girardeau County, and Carol Morrow, of Southeast Missouri State University, shared their research on the Trail of Tears in Illinois and Missouri. Marie Exler read parts of the manuscript relating to Missouri and made many helpful suggestions. The Missouri Department of Natural Resources made its research and photographs available.

Sharon Sanders of the *Southeast Missourian* searched for photographs and information. Virginia Snyder of Caledonia and Bismarck shared a copy of the diary of the Reverend Mr.

Daniel S. Buttrick, a missionary who traveled with the Cherokees on the Trail of Tears.

The Cape Girardeau and Farmington public libraries,
Ozark Regional Library in Ironton, and Springfield–Greene
County Library provided clippings and other information.
Frank Pascoe of the Missouri State Library helped greatly
with information on Missouri laws relating to Indian tribes,
and Fae Sotham of the Missouri State Historical Society in Columbia located photographs included in the book.

Beverly Baker Northup, principal chief of the Northern
Cherokee Nation, contributed information on early Cherokee
settlement west of the Mississippi River. Her interviews with
the author trace the history of the Northern Cherokee Nation
of the Old Louisiana Territory and offer insight into her work.

In Oklahoma the Cherokee Heritage Center, the Cherokee
National Museum, and the Cherokee National Historical Society in Tahlequah sent information. The Cherokee Nation
granted permission to use the nation's historic seal in the
book. Glennis Parker, longtime friend of the author, helped
with the search for information. Delores T. Sumner of the John
Vaughan Library at Northeastern State University in Tahlequah provided information on Eliza Missouri Bushyhead. The
archives department of the Oklahoma Historical Society in
Oklahoma City searched for photographic material.

The Long Distance Trails Group Office of the National Park
Service in Santa Fe, New Mexico, loaned negatives of the Trail
of Tears National Historic Trail logo.

Donald M. Lance, consultant for the Missouri Heritage
Reader series, visited Cherokee, North Carolina, and Tahlequah and other sites in Oklahoma relating to Cherokee history. He brought back books, brochures, and maps that were
very helpful.

Many thousands of words have been written about events
related to Cherokee history and the Cherokee "Trail of Tears."
The author thanks Cherokee and non-Cherokee historians
who have documented Cherokee history so well.

The Trail of Tears across Missouri

Introduction

On Tuesday evening we fell in with a detachment of the poor Cherokee Indians . . . multitudes go on foot—even aged females, apparently nearly ready to drop into the grave, were traveling with heavy burdens attached to the back—on the sometimes frozen ground, and sometimes muddy streets, with no covering for the feet except what nature had given them.

—"The Suffering Exiles: A Traveler's View
of One of the Last Emigrant Parties," by a
"Native of Maine, Traveling in the Western Country"
in the *New York Observer,* January 26, 1839

The *New York Observer* and other newspapers across the United States printed these and many other reports describing the suffering of the Cherokee Indians moving west during the winter of 1838–1839. The reports fill us with questions: Why were the Cherokees in such trouble? Where were they going? Was there no help for them? Did any of them survive the trip?

The Cherokees were in trouble because their forced move from their former homes in the southeastern United States had not been planned carefully enough. The journey to their new home west of the Mississippi River was supposed to take three months; it took more than four. Federal and state officials had been mistaken about the number of people going.

They had not taken into account the special needs of aged people, invalids, babies, and small children. Not enough wagons, teams, or horses were provided for them; there were not enough blankets or tents. Many had only summer clothing when winter came. Food was often in short supply. Promises about supplies for the trip were not kept. Promised payments for what the Cherokees had to leave behind were not made in time to help. Some settlers along the way raised prices for needed supplies and charged high tolls for crossing their lands or camping. Some even charged for burial places.

The trip from their southeastern homelands to what is now Oklahoma was almost a thousand miles. It was being made at a bad time of the year, from late fall through winter. The Cherokees on the Trail of Tears had to cross parts of five states: Tennessee, Kentucky, Illinois, Missouri, and Arkansas. And many Cherokees had been ill and weak when they set out. They had lost their homes, and many had lost all their belongings. For weeks most had been shut up in crowded government stockades. In the stockades they had seen friends and relatives sicken and die as they waited to start on the trip west.

Many government officials did not seem to care what happened to the Cherokees. They were impatient to get the Indian lands for white settlers and investors. For two decades the government had been moving Indian tribes out of the eastern and southern states. The Cherokees were among the tribes that held out the longest against moving. Their passive resistance and other tactics to shame the government had made many important officials angry.

Some people helped, or tried to help, the Cherokees. When "Indian Removal" was first discussed in Congress, many legislators and prominent citizens objected. When the removal seemed certain, missionaries and some southern whites helped in any way they could. After removal was under way, church groups often went to the camps of the traveling Indians, taking them food, clothing, and other supplies. Some storekeepers and farmers treated them fairly and kindly.

The Cherokees also had love and support along the way

This painting of Cherokees on the Trail of Tears is by Robert Lind-neux. (Woolaroc Museum, Bartlesville, Oklahoma)

from missionaries who had worked among them and came with them on the trail. These friends of the Cherokee people shared their hardships and dangers and offered as much help as they could. The doctors with each group, some contractors and interpreters, and others helping with the move did what they could. But as the weather got worse, the suffering increased.

We cannot be sure exactly how many Cherokees died in the stockades where they were held before they left or how many died on the trail. Exact records were hard to keep. Cherokee historians say more than four thousand died, about one-fourth of the tribe in the East at the time of their removal. Sadly, the forced removal also divided the Cherokee people, destroying their unity of purpose and spirit.

Few families arrived in the West with the money or the tools and animals they needed to start over. The soil and weather were very different from the fertile lands and mild climate in the Southeast. But the Cherokees were determined to build a new homeland. Within a few years, they again had churches, schools, good farms, and homes in the Indian Territory. They built one of the country's first colleges for women west of the Mississippi. Today they are the largest and one of the most successful tribes, or nations, of Native Americans. The Cherokees in Oklahoma operate schools, businesses, and social services for the benefit of tribe members. They have built the Cherokee Heritage Center near Tahlequah, Oklahoma, to preserve the history of their people.

The Eastern Band of Cherokees in North Carolina are descendants of tribe members who managed to remain in the East or who returned. They have also developed businesses and created museums and programs to tell their story.

The Cherokee people and the Cherokee culture have survived. Knowing that, we can now take a closer look at their forced exile from their ancestral homeland.

Chapter 1

The Cherokee Home in the East

The Cherokees were once the largest and most important single Indian tribe in the southeastern United States, living in the beautiful mountain areas of North and South Carolina, Georgia, Alabama, and Tennessee.

—Floyd C. Shoemaker,
Missouri Historical Review, January 1953

A television movie about the Trail of Tears might begin with a camera panning slowly across Cherokee land as it was in the early 1800s. No place in the United States was more beautiful. There were flower-covered mountains, forests with dozens of kinds of trees, open areas of rich grass, and many springs and streams.

The Cherokee people had lived on these ancestral lands for many generations before the visit of the first European in the area, Spanish explorer Hernando de Soto, in 1540. During the 1700s tribal leaders gave up parts of their territory in treaties with British officials. But at the time of the American Revolution the lands of the Cherokees extended from the eastern slopes of the Blue Ridge Mountains westward toward the Mississippi River and reached from the Ohio River almost as far south as central Georgia.

In a treaty of 1791, President George Washington's administration had guaranteed the Cherokees seventy thousand square miles of territory. Parts of the states of Georgia, North Carolina,

"In the Cherokee Mountains" is a photograph made by James Mooney in 1888. (Nineteenth Annual Report of the Bureau of American Ethnology, *1900)*

and South Carolina and areas of what later became Alabama, Tennessee, and Kentucky were included. The Cherokees gave up large parts of their hunting grounds in the treaty, but they were promised some advantages; in exchange for the land, the treaty promised them peace, the protection of the federal government, an annual payment, and tools useful for farming.

By the 1820s much more Cherokee territory had been lost by treaty. In 1817 and 1819 land in the East had been exchanged for equal acreage between the Arkansas and White Rivers for those Cherokees who had moved west. But the tribe still had large landholdings in the Southeast. Much of this land was well worked, with good farm-to-market roads. Several Cherokees had developed huge fruit orchards. Along the Great Smoky Mountains of northern Georgia, Tennessee, and North Carolina lay more than sixty Cherokee towns and villages. Most members of the tribe lived as white settlers did—in sturdy log cabins. They farmed, raised livestock, and practiced crafts such as weaving, basketry, and pottery.

Cherokees built log cabins similar to this in the 1800s.
(Oconaluftee Indian Village, Cherokee, North Carolina)

Wealthy Cherokees had brick mansions as fine as any in the East. Like white southern landowners, some held African slaves. An 1825 census of the Cherokee Nation in the East showed a population of "native Cherokee, 13,563; white men married into the Nation, 147; white women married into the Nation, 73; negro slaves, 1,277."

The Cherokee National Inventory of 1825 showed that the nation owned 17,531 cattle; 7,653 horses; 47,732 swine; 2,556 sheep; 430 goats; 752 looms; 2,486 spinning wheels; 2,948 plows; 10 sawmills; 31 gristmills; 62 blacksmith shops; 8 cotton machines; 9 stores; 6 turnpike gates; and 18 ferries. Large farms, stores, mills, and ferries had brought prosperity to many Cherokees.

Cherokee attorney John Ridge reported that his people had eighteen schools and a library of one thousand books. The Cherokees were then setting up a National Academy at New Echota, near Calhoun, Georgia. They had also started a mu-

Sequoyah invented the Cherokee syllabary to help his people learn to read and write their language. The redwood trees of California were named in his honor. (Museum of the Cherokee Indian, Cherokee, North Carolina)

seum at New Echota. As early as 1790, Cherokee leaders had decided to adopt the ways of the whites, and they had succeeded.

By the 1820s the Cherokees had a way to write their language. Sequoyah, a member of the tribe, had been fascinated to see whites exchanging messages on paper. He decided to invent a way to write the Cherokee language. Sequoyah could not read, speak, or write English, but he worked for many years to make it possible for Cherokees to read their own language. He created a writing system known as a "syllabary," in which each "letter" represents an entire syllable in the Cherokee language. Many people were suspicious of his invention, but he presented his syllabary to the Cherokee Council in 1821. Leaders soon found that both children and adults could learn to read very quickly using his method.

The tribe soon established its own newspaper, the *Cherokee Phoenix,* which published its first issue in 1828. The newspaper was printed in both Cherokee and English. It was named for the phoenix, a mythical bird that dies by diving into fire, then rises from the ashes, born anew. The *Cherokee Phoenix* had subscribers all over the United States and some in Europe. Altogether the Cherokees subscribed to eleven newspapers besides their own. Missionaries believed the number of Cherokees who could read was higher, on average, than that of their white neighbors.

The tribe had lived for many years in peace as established home owners on good farms. They sent their children to missionary schools, and so many Cherokees had accepted Christianity that they were called the "Christian tribe."

In a television program about the Trail of Tears, Cherokee leader John Ross would appear on camera very early. Ross was seven-eighths Scottish and only one-eighth Cherokee. But he had been reared among the Cherokees and considered them his people. When he came home from schools at Kingston and Maryville, Tennessee, he announced that his life would be dedicated to the tribe. In 1812 he married a full-blooded Cherokee woman, Elizabeth Brown Henley, called "Quatie" by her people. Ross proved so devoted to the Cherokees that in 1828 they chose him principal chief of the Cherokee Nation. He was to hold that office from the age of thirty-eight until his death in 1866, when he was in his seventies.

Ross spent much of his time in the 1820s and 1830s writing letters to government officials and traveling to Washington, D.C. He was trying to get assurances that his people would not be forced off their lands and sent west as some state and federal officials kept demanding.

Georgia officials were trying to force the removal of Cherokees from the state. The Cherokees were determined to hold on to their land in Georgia. In 1824 the Cherokee Council sent a delegation to Washington to gain the support of federal officials in their struggle. Leaders John Ross, George Lowrey, Elijah Hicks, and Major Ridge spent several months in the capital,

John Ross was first elected principal chief of the Cherokees in 1828. (Museum of the Cherokee Indian, Cherokee, North Carolina)

writing letters and visiting officials. One letter was so well written that legislators from Georgia accused the Cherokees of having a white "ghost writer." The Cherokees sent a statement to the *National Intelligencer* that every letter they sent was "not only written but dictated by an Indian."

They wrote over and over to President James Monroe and to other officials that the tribe would not cede any more land. The Georgians in Congress were outraged that the Indian delegation was received with the same courtesy extended to foreign diplomats. In a speech one called the Cherokees "savages" who lived on "roots, wild herbs, disgusting reptiles." When the Cherokee delegation was later seated near the Georgia representative in a restaurant, George Lowrey asked the waiter several times to bring more of a sweet-potato dish. Each time, he said in a voice loud enough for other diners to hear: "We Indians are very fond of roots!" Many in the restaurant were amused. The Georgians were only more annoyed.

Members of the Cherokee delegation won admirers in Washington with their dignity and their good manners. They were included in many social events in the capital: They attended Wednesday evening balls at the White House; a party at the home of John Calhoun, who was then secretary of war; and Tuesday evening receptions at the home of John Quincy Adams, secretary of state during the administration of President Monroe. However, when the Cherokees left the capital to return home in June 1824, President Monroe still believed it would be best if they gave up their land in Georgia. The Cherokees, however, were still determined not to give up "another foot" of their territory.

Andrew Jackson of Tennessee was elected president in 1828. Before leaving for Washington in January 1829, he gave his political blessing to one of his supporters, Sam Houston, then governor of Tennessee. Jackson hoped that Houston's planned marriage into a powerful Tennessee family would help him win reelection as governor.

Houston had lived for more than three years among the Cherokees as a young man. He had been adopted by one of their chieftains, who had given him the name "The Raven," a war title. When his new wife left him after only a few weeks of marriage, Governor Houston fled from Tennessee in disguise and went west to the home of his Cherokee family. John Jolly, then chief of the western Cherokees, took him in and made him his ambassador to Washington. Dressed in his Cherokee clothing, Houston went to visit Jackson twice on behalf of the Cherokees. The president was fond of Houston, but his appeals did not help.

Appeals from Cherokee leaders and their friends in Congress did not help, either. In 1830 Jackson pushed the Indian Removal Bill through Congress by a narrow margin. This gave the president authority to use force to remove Indians from their land if they did not go voluntarily. Sam Houston did not openly oppose removal of the eastern tribes to the West; he believed it was the best solution the Indian people could hope for. But many famous people, in and out of government, spoke out against the law and continued to speak out against Jackson's Indian policies.

David Crockett, a member of Congress from Tennessee,

Sam Houston lived among the Cherokees as a young man and was adopted by a Cherokee chief. After his marriage failed, he left Tennessee and joined his Cherokee family in the West. He went to Washington in his Cherokee clothing in the early 1830s to meet with President Jackson. (San Jacinto Museum of History, Houston, Texas)

stated: "If I'm the only member of the House to vote against this . . . the only man in the country to disapprove of it, I will . . . and glory in having done so until the day I die." Daniel Webster, senator from Massachusetts, fought the bill bitterly and advised the Cherokees to appeal to the Supreme Court.

The Cherokees' resistance to forced removal from their ancestral land was based on a sincere belief by Ross and other leaders of the tribe in the Constitution of the United States. They believed it guaranteed justice to all. Ross had called the Constitution "a beautiful document." In 1827 the Cherokee Nation had echoed its principles in creating its own constitution. They had patterned their tribal government after the government of the United States. They elected a principal chief. A

David Crockett was a congressman from Tennessee when the Indian Removal Act was passed. He spoke against the forced removal of Indians from their eastern homeland. He was defeated for a fourth term in Congress and decided to go to Texas. He died in the Battle of the Alamo in 1836. (State Historical Society of Missouri, Columbia)

second chief, a treasury officer, and others were elected to assist the chief. Two bodies of representatives went to regular meetings with the highest Cherokee officers; these were the chiefs and subchiefs each town elected.

Ross and his people also believed that their years of peace, their achievements, and their contributions gave them the right to remain on land that was legally theirs. They were convinced that all they had to do was remind enough people of their rights and they would be treated fairly. They sent many eloquent letters to officials in Jackson's administration. They published letters and articles in the *Cherokee Phoenix*, which were reprinted in newspapers across the United States. They sent pleas stating their position to the Congress, asking for justice. "In truth our cause is your own. It is the cause of liberty and justice."

Many newspapers took the side of the Cherokees in the struggle against removal. They published angry editorials, articles, and letters to the editor protesting the removal policy. The Washington reporter for the *New York Observer* noted that members of the Cherokee delegation knew more about America's laws and government than many legislators did. Cherokee delegations always included educated members of the tribe who had studied history, government, and law.

Public support of the Cherokees had its effect. In 1832 the Supreme Court ruled in the case of *Georgia v. Worcester* that states could not extend their laws over Indian territories. The Reverend Samuel A. Worcester was a teacher and a missionary at New Echota when Georgia passed a law that whites had to obtain a permit and declare an oath of allegiance to the state to remain in Cherokee Territory. Some of the missionaries either took the oath of allegiance or left the state. Worcester refused to do either and was sentenced to four years in prison.

Worcester's case was won in the Supreme Court, but when Chief Justice John Marshall announced the Court's decision, President Jackson did not change his mind. "John Marshall has made his decision," he said. "Now let him enforce it." He continued to agree with Georgia that the Cherokees should be removed. When told it would be difficult to move the Cherokees from their land, Jackson said, "Build a fire under them. When it gets hot enough, they'll go."

Jackson, the seventh president of the United States, was the first to be elected from west of the Appalachian Mountains. He had gained national fame in the Creek War of 1813–1814, which he won with the help of many Cherokees, including John Ross. He became a national hero when he won the Battle of New Orleans against the British in 1815. In the South and the new West, he was considered a man of the frontier, a man of the people.

Historians still disagree about the reasons for his Indian policies. Did Jackson hate Indians? Part of his wealth had been made in land speculation; he had once been involved in selling land that belonged to Cherokees by the treaty of 1791. But he had also adopted a three-year-old Creek boy orphaned in battle. Lincoyer, the Creek child, grew up in Jackson's home with his adopted white son and other children in the household. He was educated with the others, and when he died of tuberculosis in 1827 he was buried as a member of the family.

Jackson often met with Indian delegations. He expressed concern and sympathy for their cause; but he supported the eastern states in their demands that tribes in the East be moved west of the Mississippi River. In the struggle between Georgia and the Cherokees, he was on Georgia's side.

As a military commander during the Creek War of 1813–1814, Jackson had been glad to accept the Cherokees' help in battles with the Creeks. To their surprise, this meant nothing to him later. He sometimes treated Cherokee tribal leaders with special bitterness.

One chieftain named Junaluska went to him on behalf of the Cherokees. Junaluska had saved Jackson's life during the Battle of Horseshoe Bend against the Creeks, but the president cut him off abruptly, saying, "Sir, your audience is at an end. I cannot help you."

As his second term began in 1832, Jackson promised to get the Indian Removal Bill enforced. The Choctaws had signed the Treaty of Dancing Rabbit Creek in 1830, giving up all their land east of the Mississippi River. The Chickasaws, the Creeks, and the Seminoles signed removal treaties in 1832. The Cherokees held out, hoping their friend Henry Clay would be the next president. But Martin Van Buren, Jackson's vice president, won the election of 1836.

At first Indian leaders thought Van Buren would be easier to deal with than Jackson. He did agree to give them a little longer to prepare for removal. But he soon refused to see Chief Ross. He refused to consider a petition signed by most of the tribe.

Both federal and state governments were pushing harder for Cherokee removal. Word of the gold fields in northwest Georgia had spread, and more and more whites were moving into Cherokee lands.

Government officials promised to pay for tribal land. They promised that individuals would be paid for whatever they had to leave behind. They assured the Cherokees that generous amounts of land awaited them in the West. Food and transportation for the trip would be supplied. Everyone who went would receive basic equipment for starting over in a new land. They would be given one year's living expenses. Those who went voluntarily would get special benefits. Deadlines for removal were set. Still the Cherokees held out.

Chapter 2

Countdown to Removal

When told . . . no alternative remained to them as a nation but death or removal, they seemed not to hesitate saying, "It is death anyhow. We may as well die here. . . ." They cling to the graves of their fathers and say, "Let us die with them . . . if we leave this country, these hills and vales, this mountain air, we shall sicken and die."

—From a letter written by Sophia Sawyer,
New Echota, Georgia, 1832

Some Cherokees had settled west of the Mississippi River both before and after the American Revolution. The Louisiana Territory had been transferred from France to Spain in 1762. Spain traded it back to France in 1800, and in 1803 the United States bought the territory from France. A Cherokee historian believes that by the time of the Louisiana Purchase there were six thousand Cherokees living in what is now southeast Missouri and northeast Arkansas. Many had settled along the St. Francis River to farm and hunt.

Cherokees continued to emigrate west after the Louisiana Purchase. Both state and federal officials, including President Thomas Jefferson, wanted to trade land west of the Mississippi River for Indian lands in the East. The settlements in southeast Missouri attracted some of those who decided to move west. Others went on to present-day northwest Arkansas.

Cherokees had settled in southeast Missouri long before the Trail of Tears. Cherokee historians believe that they had settled in what are now Cape Girardeau, Perry, Bollinger, Scott, Mississippi, and New Madrid Counties. (courtesy of the Northern Cherokee Nation of the Old Louisiana Territory)

Over a thousand members of the Chickamauga band moved to the area near Dardanelle, Arkansas, in 1808 at the suggestion of President Thomas Jefferson.

During the winter of the New Madrid earthquakes of 1811–1812 many of the Cherokees in southeast Missouri and northeast Arkansas moved west to the area between the Arkansas and the White Rivers. By the treaty of 1817 the Cherokee Nation ceded land in the East for an equal amount in the Arkansas region for members of the tribe who had settled there. The same year the government established Fort Smith on the Arkansas River, partly to keep the peace between the Cherokees and the Osage Indians in northwestern Arkansas.

President Monroe's administration continued to favor the

*Fort Smith was established on the Arkansas River in 1817 to protect
trappers, hunters, and explorers and keep the peace between the Osage
Indians and the Cherokees. By 1819 the fort had "two block houses
and lines of cabins or barracks," according to English explorer
Thomas Nuttall. (Arkansas History Commission, Little Rock)*

removal of the Indians from the East, and more Cherokees
went west in the 1820s. The president's policy did not make
sense to the Cherokees, and one writer recorded their argu-
ments: "A few years ago he sent them a plow & a hoe—said it
was not good . . . to hunt—they must cultivate the earth. Now
he tells them there is good hunting at the Arkansas: if they go
there he will give them rifles." Fearful of losing everything,
some took the government's offer and moved.

During Jackson's administrations the relentless efforts for
removal increased, and still more of the Cherokees left, some
singly, some in family groups. One of the most important
groups to decide to leave was led by the powerful Ridge family. The head of the family, "The Ridge," had fought with Jack-

son against the Creeks and earned the rank of major in the American army.

Major Ridge was unschooled, but he had a brilliant mind and had become very wealthy. He sent his son John to law school so the tribe would have a good attorney. He supported the work of Sequoyah, a distant relative, who invented a way to write the Cherokee language. Ridge also helped start the *Cherokee Phoenix,* the national Cherokee newspaper. His nephew, Elias Boudinot, raised funds for the paper and became its first editor. Major Ridge was an enthusiastic supporter of Cherokee schools. He helped many young people of the nation—both girls and boys—go to college.

At the beginning of the fight against removal, and for a long time, the Ridge family firmly supported Chief Ross. They went on trips to Washington to present the Cherokee case to Congress and the president. They believed the nation should not give up any more of its land. Some of the best letters written for the Cherokees' claims to their lands were written by John Ridge.

But at some point the Ridges decided that the struggle to keep the Cherokee lands in the East was a lost cause. Major Ridge had been one of the first to recognize that Indians had no hope against whites in war. Now he and his relatives and supporters realized they could not win with words either. Two factions developed within the tribe—the majority, who supported Chief Ross in his struggle to keep their homeland in the East; and the "Treaty Group," who thought the only solution left to them was to emigrate to the lands in the West.

In 1828 a treaty had been signed in Washington between the government and the chiefs and headmen of the Cherokee Nation living west of the Mississippi River. This treaty had "guaranteed forever" 7 million acres in the West as a permanent home for the Cherokees, both those already in the West and those still east of the Mississippi River. The treaty promised that the nation would "never in all future time be embarrassed by having . . . placed over it the jurisdiction of a Territory or a state. . . ."

Major Ridge signed the Treaty of New Echota, agreeing to exchange the Cherokee homeland in the East for land west of the Mississippi River. (Museum of the Cherokee Indian, Cherokee, North Carolina)

Rather than lose all they had to the states in the East, which were taking over Cherokee ancestral lands, the Ridge party signed the Treaty of New Echota in December 1835. The treaty conveyed to the United States all lands owned, claimed, or possessed by the Cherokee Nation east of the Mississippi River. Major Ridge was the tribe's most impressive orator. He explained his decision to give up the Cherokee homeland:

I am one of the native sons of these wild woods. I have hunted the deer and turkey here, more than fifty years. I have fought your battles. . . . I know the Indians have an older title. . . . We obtained the land from the living God above . . . yet they are strong and we are weak. We are few, they are many. We cannot stay here in safety and comfort. . . . We can never forget these homes. . . . I would willingly

Senators Henry Clay, Daniel Webster, and John C. Calhoun were opposed to the ratification of the Treaty of New Echota. (State Historical Society of Missouri, Columbia)

die to preserve them, but any forcible effort to keep them will cost us our lands, our lives and the lives of our children.

Since by Cherokee law the tribe owned all land in common, no individual or minority group had a right to dispose of it. The penalty was death, and many years earlier Major Ridge had helped enforce this law. As he signed the Treaty of New Echota, he said, "This is my death warrant." His nephew, Elias Boudinot, also spoke of the death penalty he expected for signing the treaty. "I know I take my life in my hand . . . but the great Cherokee Nation will be saved. . . . [W]hat is a man worth who will not dare to die for his people?"

Army officer Major William Davis, assigned to enroll the Cherokees for removal, wrote the secretary of war that "nine-tenths" of the Cherokees would instantly reject the Treaty of New Echota: "That paper called a treaty is no treaty at all." Friends in Washington assured John Ross that the treaty would never be ratified. It was bitterly attacked by Senator John Calhoun of South Carolina and Senator Daniel Webster of Massachusetts. On May 17, 1836, however, the Senate ratified the

Treaty of New Echota by one vote. On May 23 President Jackson signed the treaty into law. The deadline for removal of all the Cherokees from the East was set for May 23, 1838.

A public outcry arose. Government officials opposed to forced removal, private citizens, and many newspapers protested the government action. Former president John Quincy Adams of Massachusetts, who had been elected to the House of Representatives by his state, called the action of the Senate "infamous . . . a disgrace to the nation's history." Henry Clay, senator from Kentucky, quoted what Jefferson had said about slavery: "Indeed, I tremble for my country when I reflect that God is just, and that His justice cannot sleep forever."

Ralph Waldo Emerson, the New England writer, sent a long letter to President Martin Van Buren. The newspapers had reported that a majority of Cherokees had rejected the Treaty of New Echota, "15,668 out of 18,000 souls," he had read. Yet,

the American president and the Cabinet, the Senate and the House of Representatives, neither hear these men nor see them, and are contracting to put this active nation into carts and boats, and to drag them over mountains and rivers at a vast distance beyond the Mississippi. . . . Sir, does the government think the people of the United States are become savage and mad? . . . You, sir, will bring down that chair on which you sit; and the name of this nation . . . will stink to the world.

"Removal" was not a word John Ross could accept, but the holdouts to removal were in a struggle they could not win. Since the early 1830s Georgia policies had encouraged the harassment of the Cherokees. The federal government did nothing to protect them. This was part of Jackson's plan to "build a fire under them."

Laws had been changed so that Cherokees had no rights in Georgia courts. Indians could not sue or testify against whites. The Cherokee Legislative Council was prohibited from meeting—unless the meeting was to plan for removal. Cherokees who spoke against removal were subject to arrest. White settlers were free to take horses and carriages from Cherokees on the road. They could cut the Cherokees' wood, harvest their crops, and vandalize their places of business.

Finally all Indian land was declared the property of the state and sold by lottery. Buyers were not supposed to take possession immediately, but many did. The prosperous homes, farms, and businesses of the tribal leaders were taken quickly by the lottery winners. John Ross sued in federal court to retain his property; but he returned from Washington in April 1833 to find strangers living in his home. They were operating his farm and ferry and selling his animals and produce. His wife, Quatie, a semi-invalid, and their youngest children were living in two rooms of the house until his return.

The principal chief of the Cherokees could do nothing except take his family across the Tennessee border, where his ancestors had always lived. He was living there in a log home when John Howard Payne visited him. We know Payne as the composer of the famous song "Home, Sweet Home." He was also a respected playwright of his time and wrote for magazines and newspapers. He had decided to establish a magazine in London, and he wanted to write about Cherokee history and culture. He visited Chief Ross to study old Cherokee documents and interview elders of the tribe.

Payne believed that if people only knew about Cherokee history and achievements, they would not allow the removal. But while he was staying in the Ross home, the Georgia Guard crossed the border into Tennessee and arrested both men. Ross and Payne were kept in prison for more than a week under very bad conditions. The *Cherokee Phoenix* had been seized by the Georgia Guard and the Ridge faction a few days before the arrests. The Cherokee people had lost their chief and their voice.

After the men were released from prison, however, the outraged Payne became a voice for the Cherokees, trying to make people understand what was happening to them. The *Knoxville Register* and other newspapers carried his articles, and his words influenced many readers. But Georgia continued its ef-

Type for the Cherokee syllabary was cast in Boston and shipped to New Echota in early 1828. The Georgia Guard removed the press that printed the Cherokee Phoenix *in 1835. (Museum of the Cherokee Indian, Cherokee, North Carolina)*

forts to pressure the president to carry out the removal. Missionaries and others were arrested, accused of encouraging Cherokee resistance. There was no help from the federal government. The secretary of war said he could do nothing because the Senate had ratified the treaty; the Senate tabled Cherokee petitions; and President Van Buren refused to meet with Chief Ross or to grant a delay.

Those who had signed the New Echota treaty prepared to leave. In January 1837 about six hundred wealthy members of the Treaty Party emigrated west with slaves, horses, and "droves of oxen." They traveled overland, and white observers noted they were "well mounted, well dressed, and well fed." They had fine saddle horses and cattle. Strong draft teams pulled dozens of big wagons loaded with furniture and other belongings. The impressive show of wealth this group made was to cause more trouble for the Cherokees who came later:

Most of them would be forced on the long trail without the supplies and equipment needed for such a trip, but landowners believed the Cherokees had plenty of "government money." Some settlers along the way would try to get their share of it.

Chapter 3

Forced Removal Begins

The whole scene since I have been in this country has been nothing but a heartrending one. . . . If I could, and I could not do them a greater kindness, I would remove every Indian tomorrow beyond the reach of the white men, who, like vultures, are watching, ready to pounce upon their prey and strip them of everything they have.

—General Ellis Wool in *Indian Removal,* by Grant Foreman

Forced removal did not begin with the Cherokees. Beginning in the early 1830s Indian tribes in the Southeast had been forced to give up their homes and move west. The Choctaw, the Creek, the Chickasaw, the Seminole, and the Cherokee were called the "Five Civilized Tribes" because many had adopted white ways. Many had become Christians and lived settled lives, farming as their white neighbors did. Members of all the Five Civilized Tribes had been pressured to trade their land in the East for western lands.

The Choctaw leaders were the first to sign a treaty after the passage of the Indian Removal Act, the Treaty of Dancing Rabbit Creek. A French writer, Alexis de Tocqueville, happened to be in Memphis in the winter of 1831–1832 when a group of Choctaws passed through on their way west.

It was then the middle of winter, and the cold was unusually severe; the snow had frozen hard upon the ground, and the river was drift-

ing huge masses of ice. The Indians had their families with them,
and they brought . . . the wounded and sick, with children newly
born and old men upon the verge of death. They possessed neither
tents nor wagons, but only their arms and some provisions. I saw
them embark to pass the mighty river and never will that solemn
spectacle fade. . . . No cry, no sob was heard among the assembled
crowd; all was silent.

De Tocqueville predicted that the Indians would not find
the good life they had been promised beyond the Mississippi
River. "The countries . . . are inhabited by other tribes, which
will receive them with jealous hostility. . . . Hunger is in the
rear, war awaits them, and misery besets them on all sides."

The removal of the Five Civilized Tribes took place as
rapidly as the government could get the necessary treaties
signed. The Choctaws emigrated in 1831–1832; the Creeks were
forced to move in 1836; the Chickasaws migrated peacefully
in 1837–1838; the Seminoles waged war to keep their homeland from 1836 to 1843, but their forced removal to Creek Territory began in 1836. Some Cherokees started emigrating in
1837, and their forced removal began in 1838.

In March 1837 the Ridges set out from their homes, taking
many relatives and supporters with them. This was the first
group of Cherokees to be moved by the government under the
terms of the New Echota treaty. They traveled partly by flat-
boat and keelboat, partly overland. Dr. John S. Young, the
"conducting agent," was in charge of the trip, with three as-
sistants, a doctor, and three interpreters.

According to records kept by Dr. Young and the doctor,
there were 466 in the Ridge group. Half of them were children.
The boats were damp and cold, and the doctor reported many
people ill from colds, flu, measles, and fever. He also treated
toothaches, injuries from accidents, and wounds from the
fighting that sometimes broke out among the young men. In
spite of many delays, the group reached Arkansas by the end
of March. Major Ridge and his family were put ashore near
Fort Smith to go overland. They planned to settle on Honey

Creek, near the Missouri border. Others in the group went on to Fort Coffee, near the village of Scullyville, where the Choctaws received their government annuities.

Another group of about 360 Cherokees started overland in October 1837, led by government guide B. B. Cannon. The Cannon group crossed the Hiwassee River near Calhoun, Georgia, on October 14. According to Cannon's report, they usually "marched" as much as fifteen to twenty miles a day, with little rest. On October 25 they stopped briefly to bury a child. On October 27 their contracting agent left and returned home, claiming poor health. Cannon had to appoint another agent to obtain needed supplies. For most of the trip he was able to issue "corn and fodder" for the animals and cornmeal and bacon for the people, but sometimes supplies were scarce.

After only a week Cannon wrote that "the Indians appear fatigued." But it was not until a week later that they stopped for a day to wash clothes, repair wagons, and shoe horses. This first stop was at Nashville, and some of the leaders went to visit the man they called "General Jackson," now retired from the presidency to his home near Nashville.

The travelers suffered many hardships as the weather got worse. They were delayed for two days at the Ohio River because of high winds and at the Mississippi River where many became ill. Letters and messages sent back from the Cannon group about deaths, illnesses, lack of supplies, delays, and other problems made the Cherokees still in the East even more reluctant to start west. Reports from those who reached the Indian Territory described a strange and different land. Most of the soil there had never been broken and was tightly webbed with the strong roots of buffalo grass. The area already held thousands of Indians of other tribes as well as "Old Settlers," the Cherokees who had moved much earlier. As Alexis de Tocqueville had predicted, many were not eager to share space with the newcomers.

All the reports from the West strengthened the resolve of Cherokees still in the East to stand their ground. They could not believe the government would really force them to leave.

Andrew Jackson returned to his home near Nashville after his second term as president. Several Cherokee leaders traveling with the B. B. Cannon detachment in 1837 visited him there. (State Historical Society of Missouri, Columbia)

Chief Ross encouraged them to stay in their homes and start their crops. Their shock when they were forcibly taken from their homes was among the causes of their suffering. Historians believe these last Cherokees to leave, those who were removed by force, are the ones who called their journey the "Trail of Tears." In the Cherokee language it was the "trail where we cried."

John G. Burnett, a Tennessee soldier who spoke the Cherokee language, had been sent as an interpreter to the "Smoky Mountain Country." He witnessed, he later wrote, "the execution of the most brutal order in the History of American Warfare," as forced removal began. "In May 1838 an army of four thousand regulars, and three thousand volunteer soldiers under command of General Winfield Scott, marched into the Indian country and wrote the blackest chapter on the pages of American History."

As the May 1838 deadline for removal approached, the gov-

Private John Burnett wrote "The Cherokee Removal through the Eyes of a Private Soldier" in 1890, when he was eighty years old. "I wish I could forget it all," he wrote, "but the memory of six hundred and forty-five wagons lumbering over the frozen ground with their Cargo of suffering humanity still lingers in my memory." This photograph shows Private Burnett and his second wife, Rebecca Moss Burnett. (Museum of the Cherokee Indian, Cherokee, North Carolina)

ernment had sent soldiers to build stockades to hold Cherokees who would not agree to remove themselves. In a letter to John Howard Payne, William S. Coodey wrote: "The entire Cherokee population were captured by the U.S. troops under General Scott in 1838 and marched . . . upon the border of Tennessee where they were encamped in large bodies until the time of their final removal west."

Some soldiers ordered to carry out the forced removal refused. General R. D. Dunlap, commander of Tennessee volunteer soldiers, took his troops home when they were told to help build stockades. He stated he would not "dishonor the Tennessee arms" in this way.

And General Ellis Wool asked to be relieved of his command rather than have to enforce removal. He had risked the anger of President Jackson earlier by sending him a resolution by the Cherokees stating that the Treaty of New Echota was not valid. The president informed the general that he was insulting the commander in chief and the American people. General Wool refused to be a part of the removal anymore, writing, "They are being robbed and plundered . . . subjected to every species of oppression . . . ninety-nine out of a hundred of them will go penniless to the West."

Wool's replacement, General Winfield Scott, had a reputation for fairness and compassion. But he was a soldier who did not question orders. On May 10 he sent an address to the Cherokee people "remaining in North Carolina, Georgia, Tennessee, and Alabama":

The President of the United States has sent me, with a powerful army, to cause you, in obedience to the treaty of 1835, to join that part of your people who are already established in prosperity, on the other side of the Mississippi. . . . The full moon of May is already on the wane, and before another shall have passed away, every Cherokee man, woman, and child, in these states, must be in motion to join their brethren in the far West.

He urged the "Chiefs, headmen, and warriors" to spare him the horror of "witnessing the destruction of the Cherokees." He urged the people to gather at Ross's Landing or Gunter's Landing ready to depart. He promised they would be "received in kindness," would be provided with food and clothing, and would be transported "at their ease" and "in comfort" to their new home.

On May 23, 1838, he put his force of seven thousand soldiers to the task of rounding up Cherokees who had not left their homes. Scott ordered his officers to be kind. People were to have plenty of time to pack belongings. He ordered special consideration for the aged, the ill, pregnant women, and small children.

Some soldiers obeyed his orders. Perhaps most did. But there were many sad exceptions. People were often rushed out of their homes with nothing but the clothes they wore, denied time to pack for the trip. Time was not always allowed to get

This scene from "Unto These Hills" shows an actor portraying Juna-
luska in the final scene of the drama. Junaluska returned to North
Carolina after emigrating west on the Trail of Tears. The general assem-
bly granted him state citizenship and a tract of land in the mountains
of Cherokee County. ("Unto These Hills," Cherokee, North Carolina)

children in from play or work. Husbands came home to find
families gone.

Years later, on his eightieth birthday, John Burnett wrote
sadly about what he saw. "Men working in the fields were arrested and driven to the stockade. Women were dragged from
their homes by soldiers whose language they could not understand. Children were often separated from their parents and
driven into the stockades with the sky for a blanket and the
earth for a pillow. The old and the infirm were prodded with
bayonets to hurry them to the stockade." He told of one "frail"
widow with a new baby and two small children. The woman
had to set out with her baby on her back and holding a small
child with each hand. After several miles of walking, she fell

and died in the road. Burnett wrote that Chief Junaluska, who had saved Jackson's life in the Creek War, had "tears gushing down his cheeks" at the scene. ". . . if I had known at the battle of the Horse Shoe what I know now," he said, "American History would have been differently written."

At best, people being herded along by the soldiers might be hit or pricked with bayonets if they had trouble keeping up. One report tells of mounted soldiers acting as if they were driving cattle. They rode in circles around the people, hooting and shouting insults, raising choking dust.

Another writer described people being forced through water by mounted soldiers. They arrived at the stockade with shoes ruined and nothing dry to wear.

In June, Scott announced that he had fifteen thousand Cherokees in his stockades. Some stockades were so crowded people had hardly more than a spot on the ground where they could sit.

Naturally, conditions soon became very unhealthy. With a limited water supply, sanitation was poor. Children and old people began dying almost at once from exhaustion, shock, and poor food. Many diseases broke out.

From some stockades the Cherokees could go to bathe in the streams, to hunt for food, or to look for medicinal herbs. Others could not leave for any reason. Everything depended on the whims of the officer in charge.

General Scott's first attempt to move three groups west in June 1838, using military conductors, resulted in many deaths. Travelers went partly by boat, partly by train, partly overland. It was a drought year. The emigrants could not find the water and grass their animals needed along the way. Local food supplies were so scarce that there was little the Cherokees could buy. Heat and road dust created more health problems. Many fell ill and died. Accidents on the water took other lives. Some Cherokees escaped and went back home.

The suffering of these groups was so obvious that Scott received complaints from onlookers. More than sixty citizens of Athens, Georgia, signed a protest. So did people living in Monroe and Blount Counties in Georgia.

In the end the largest group of Cherokees removed themselves. John Ross and other leaders took responsibility for the move in order to wait until cooler weather.

General Scott agreed to let the tribe manage its own move. He appointed Chief Ross's brother, Lewis, as commissary. This meant Lewis Ross would contract for supplies for people and livestock to be delivered regularly along the trail at government expense. The Cherokees could use their own unarmed police force, called "Light Horse," to keep marchers in order and help them in various ways.

Control over their trip gave the remaining Cherokees some advantages; it also left them open to blame for some of the problems that occurred. Probably most of the Cherokee people preferred taking their chances with their own leaders in command. But one serious problem resulted. The government money promised for expenses did not flow as quickly to Cherokee leaders as it would have to U.S. military officers. Tribe members and leaders often spent their own funds, for which they were never fully repaid.

The Cherokees also lacked access to some important information that those involved with earlier groups had sent to government officials. Countless lives might have been saved by a letter written to the Bureau of Indian Affairs in January 1838 by G. S. Townsend, an attending physician to the group B. B. Cannon had led west the year before.

Dr. Townsend strongly warned against making the trip overland, both for economic reasons and for the comfort and safety of the Cherokees. He blamed delays at river crossings for causing the serious illnesses that two-thirds of the group he attended suffered. While waiting to cross rivers, he wrote, people had to breathe "the miasmas" of the swamps and had only bad water to drink.

Dr. Townsend suggested that future emigrants be taken by boat to Boonville, Missouri, where the approach to the river was not swampy. From there the overland route to the Indian Territory would be much more comfortable than the route through the southern part of the state. He also suggested using

Missouri River. (photograph by Mark Sullivan, courtesy Missouri Department of Conservation)

oxen to pull the wagons because they could better survive on available forage than horses; oxen could also more easily bear the stresses of the trip.

As if to make sure his suggestions would be considered, Townsend repeated several times that the government could save money and effort by his suggestion. Perhaps few officials ever saw his letter to C. A. Harris at the Bureau of Indian Affairs. His warnings were not heeded.

Chapter 4

The Trail of Tears

We are now about to take our final leave and kind farewell to our native land, the country that the great spirit gave our Fathers. . . . It is with sorrow that we are forced by the . . . white man to quit the scenes of our childhood . . . we bid a farewell to all we hold dear.
—George Hicks to John Ross,
from the *Papers of Chief John Ross*, November 1838

Many years after the Cherokee removal General Scott wrote in his autobiography that the Cherokees "took their way, if not rejoicing, at least in comfort." He admitted that they had experienced many of the miseries of life but believed "hope—a worldly, as well as a Christian's hope cheered them on." Other observers did not see much hope in the faces of the Cherokees as they prepared to leave.

In Tennessee

For most of the Cherokees on the Trail of Tears, the trip began in Tennessee. They assembled at Rattlesnake Spring, near what is now Charleston, Tennessee. Historian Grant Foreman reports they had 645 wagons, 5,000 horses, and a large number of oxen.

The people were divided into groups of approximately one thousand. Each group had a conductor, or leader, with guides, wagon masters, commissaries, farriers to shoe horses, black-smiths, and two doctors. Gaps of a few days were to be left between the departures of the groups. This was planned to give contractors time to take provisions to where they would be needed on the trail.

Some Cherokees had managed to keep their animals. Some were riding or driving their own horses and using their own vehicles loaded with belongings. Some may have been able to do this in exchange for early promises to go when everything was ready. For others, white friends may have taken care of livestock, wagons, and belongings until it was time to leave.

The Cherokees could hunt as they traveled. Those who had money could buy whatever was available from farmers and stores. They could let their animals graze at night. But this would not be enough. They and their animals would need extra provisions. Contractors were hired to see that the provisions were delivered along the way.

Records of when each group started on the trip do not agree, but several witnesses reported on the departure of one early detachment. It was a group of 1,103 people conducted by John Benge. The day was sunny and beautiful, but the Cherokees felt only a great sadness at leaving their homeland. They were at last free of the stockades, but they were facing an unknown future. After prayer led by John Ross, they moved off silently, with no singing or conversation.

John Burnett wrote that children stood up in the wagons and waved good-bye to their mountain homes as they left. Most of the people were in summer clothing, many barefoot. William S. Coodey, a nephew of John Ross, later wrote to John Howard Payne of a sign in the sky as the word was given to move on. "At this very moment a low sound of distant thunder fell on my ear. In almost an exact western direction a dark spiral cloud was rising above the horizon. . . . The sun was unclouded—no rain fell—the thunder rolled away. . . . It was . . . looked upon as omens of some future event in the west."

The movement of thousands of Cherokees looked like an

Men, women, and children reenact the forced move of the Cherokees west in 1838. ("Unto These Hills," Cherokee, North Carolina)

army on the march. Wagons were in the center. The Light Horse rode along the lines, and as the detachments started soldiers rode at the flanks and rear to make sure the group kept moving and nobody turned back.

The government provided one wagon for every twenty people, one saddle horse for every four. Wagons carried belongings, the old, the ill, the disabled, and small children. Women with babies on their backs sometimes rode horses. Often they held two or more children on horseback with them. Able-bodied women, men, and older children walked beside the wagons that held their family members and possessions.

Mounted men rode alongside the wagons part of the time. They also scouted out camping places for the night and explored the route to be covered the next day. They acted as general troubleshooters.

This seemingly good plan would break down as the miles

passed. When animals and wagons were lost, remaining wagons grew more crowded. Many who were old or ill gave up their places in the wagons to someone in greater need. Survivors of the Trail of Tears often recalled they walked every step of the way.

One group of Cherokees was conducted by Elijah Hicks, a brother-in-law of Chief Ross. In the place of honor at the head of the group rode a seventy-six-year-old chieftain named White Path, who was much loved by his people. White Path had fought with Jackson in the Creek War. He had opposed the Cherokee constitution, but he had later been a member of the Cherokee Council and a delegate to Washington.

White Path was in poor health, and everyone urged him to ride in a wagon. But he felt that it would cheer his people to see him ahead of them on his old pony. He wanted to remind the tribe that whatever they had lost, they still had their history and their traditions.

The other groups left on schedule. John Ross stayed behind until the last, to supervise departures and receive reports from those on the road.

On October 16, leader J. Powell wrote to Ross from Blythe's Ferry, Tennessee, to report delays. They had arrived at the ferry early the day before, but only twenty wagons were taken across the Tennessee River that day. Powell said ferry operators seemed to want to hold them back. He thought they did this for the benefit, or "lucrative purpose," of nearby residents. Probably local people were selling the Cherokees food and other supplies and wanted them in the area as long as possible.

Later Powell wrote Ross that on the second day four ferry boats ran from dawn to dark. They got forty vehicles across, leaving eighteen for the third day. Powell did not mention whether or not livestock and horses could swim the Tennessee River. At calm and shallow streams, wagons could be floated across behind swimming teams. This practice could be dangerous, however.

Groups faced delays, extra expenses, and danger at every river. Often teams and wagons loaded with possessions were lost. If a team panicked, or the current took control of a wagon, people could drown in the struggle to save their possessions.

Few of the reports sent back to Ross had good news. Evan Jones, a Welsh missionary conducting a group, wrote from McMinnville that on October 16 his group had traveled sixteen miles. But they were so tired they planned to camp for several days before going on. He was angry that the blankets, shoes, and winter clothing promised them had not arrived.

On October 16, Elijah Hicks sent a disturbing report from Nashville. Five of his people had died. Forty or fifty more were ill, and he feared more deaths. Most of the travelers badly needed warmer clothing. Among the very ill was White Path, who had started off so bravely. He believed the old chief could not last long.

Hicks had been warned that beyond Nashville the roads would get worse. The passage of many hooves and wheels made roads rough; deep ruts developed. Passengers in the wagons had a jolting ride. This could be a matter of life and death for the sick. As wheels, hooves, and feet cut road surfaces, the trail became like a streambed deep in mud. Animals floundered and fell. Vehicles got stuck. The fall rains had started, and some roads soon became running creeks.

Hicks wrote of the days spent getting through the Cumberland Mountains. The travelers had to use double teams to get wagons up the slopes. That meant long delays to bring horses back down so they could pull more wagons up.

Hicks and other conductors faced another serious problem: White merchants followed the train with liquor for sale. Hicks wrote that one of his Light Horse police, Nocowee, had "given himself up" to liquor. He had been uselessly drunk for days and at times had to be driven along the trail in chains.

Hicks complained about the high tolls that were charged the wagon train. Some large landowners demanded payment from Cherokees for crossing their land, and rates changed from place to place. Crossing the mountains Hicks had to pay forty dollars for the whole group. At other places it was seventy-five cents per wagon, fifteen cents per horse. Leaders had been given money for tolls and ferries, but they had expected much lower costs.

Sometimes local people demanded pay for damage that had not happened. The Cherokees had to pay because they could not prove their people had not caused the damage claimed. Reports show conductors were worried about how long money for expenses would last. Claims made against individuals were also worrisome. If they had no money, they often had to give their accusers an animal or other property. George Hicks wrote: "since we have been on our march many of us have been stopped and our horses taken from our Teams for the payment of unjust and past Demands. Yet the government says you must go, and its citizens say you must pay me. . . . [O]ur property has been stolen and robbed by white men and no means given us to pay our debts."

Jesse Bushyhead, a Cherokee Baptist minister who was leading members of his church and others, confirmed the problems in a letter of October 21. "Our property is robbed from us," he wrote. "We are in a defenseless position." The Light Horse had no authority over anyone but Cherokees. The soldiers had no authority over white civilians, and some had no interest in the Indians beyond getting them to the Indian Territory.

Evan Jones had written the week before that he had passed the Bushyhead group, which was stalled because their oxen were sick—they had eaten poisonous plants. And the Reverend Bushyhead had other serious worries on his mind. Some of those contracted to supply food for people and animals were not delivering it on schedule. Arriving late, it caused hunger. Arriving early, it forced the Cherokees to discard possessions so wagons could be used to carry supplies.

Worse problems were ahead for the travelers. Farther along the trail, suppliers sometimes left spoiled meat. It had to be quickly burned to keep hungry people from eating it. Sometimes cornmeal was full of worms. Sometimes hay was moldy and could not be used for fear animals would sicken and die. Bushyhead asked for permission to buy another team and wagon. He explained that it took twelve wagons to carry a

The Reverend Jesse Bushyhead, a Cherokee Baptist minister, led a detachment west on the Trail of Tears. This photograph is from a painting by Charles Bird King. (Archives and Manuscripts Division of the Oklahoma Historical Society)

three-day supply of food for the humans and livestock in his group.

He wrote again on October 26. His people were concerned about the pay the government had promised for their property left behind in the East. They were embarrassed about their debts to others in the group, and they wanted to be sure that their claims had not been lost. They needed to know that they would receive the money due them for their homes, mills, cattle, and other property.

Evan Jones had observed that Bushyhead was having trouble with "the discontents" in his group, but the Reverend Bushyhead assured Ross that everyone was trying to stay in good spirits in spite of worries and problems. All wanted to get the trip over as soon as possible. They all hoped "by good morals and friendly deportment to obtain the good will and kindness of white brothers."

In Kentucky

As they went into Kentucky, the Cherokees could have told themselves: "This used to belong to us." The Ohio River formed the northern border of land they had once held. It now formed Kentucky's border.

After repeated ceding of land to the United States, the original homeland of the Cherokee Nation had become smaller and smaller. Now it was gone altogether. They were walking the Trail of Tears so others could have those parts of Georgia, Alabama, Tennessee, and North Carolina that had once been their homeland.

Another traveler in Kentucky at the time published a description of the Cherokees on the trail. The writer called himself "A Native of Maine, Traveling in the Western Country." He came upon the front part of a Cherokee train that was just pitching tents for the night in a cold rain and wind.

The train filled the road for three miles. Some of the group were on horseback, but most were on foot. People who lived near the roads where Indians passed told him the Cherokees buried fourteen or fifteen bodies at every stopping place.

The writer met the Reverend Jesse Bushyhead and reported with surprise: "They will not travel on the Sabbath. . . . When the Sabbath came, they must stop, and not merely stop—they must worship. . . ." He observed that Cherokee faces reflected every feeling but happiness. "Some have a downcast, dejected look . . . others a wild frantic appearance. . . . Most of them seemed intelligent and refined."

He told of one woman riding in a carriage with her husband. She held a dying child about three years old. He imagined the grief she must feel. She would have to bury her child by the side of the road and go on the next day. The writer admitted: "I turned from the sight with feelings words cannot express and wept. . . ."

He recalled President Van Buren's announcement to Congress in December 1838 that the Cherokees had left their homeland "with no apparent reluctance." The president reported that the removal "had been completed with praiseworthy humanity . . . with the happiest effects." The first detachment was at that time still not halfway to Indian Territory. The writer wished the president could have stood with him in Kentucky that day. He would have seen that "many of the aged Indians were suffering extremely from . . . fatigue. Several quite ill, one aged man . . . in the last struggles of death."

The weather had been cold in Tennessee, but it was much worse in Kentucky, with cold rain or snow. The Cherokees could hope for nothing better. They were traveling into winter, a winter different from the mild season of their old home. Most Cherokees had spent their whole lives in the southern states. They were shocked at how harsh late fall weather could be.

Near Hopkinsville, on the Nashville Road, the Cherokees stopped to hold White Path's funeral. They had made a white wooden box to cover his grave. They raised a white flag so other detachments would know who lay there. Groups that followed made the grave a shrine. They paused to rest, to pray, and to remember their departed leader. Buried beside White Path was a village leader named Fly Smith.

On November 13 another detachment camped near Hopkinsville. There, according to more than one writer, citizens brought donations for their comfort. Such help is not mentioned often. But church groups sometimes met the train with food, blankets, and warm clothing. Some denominations had carried out missionary work for decades in the Cherokee Nation, and their congregations heard about the removal in their churches.

There were examples of kindness in Kentucky recorded by conductors. A woman who was ready to give birth stayed behind with two friends and made a little camp. They planned to catch up with the others later. Though the women had supplies, the conductor wrote, "People who lived nearby took care of them."

There were also examples of needless sorrow. About ten miles from the Ohio River in Kentucky, a young woman who had given birth a few days before was found dead with her infant in her arms. The Reverend Daniel Buttrick, a missionary emigrating with the Cherokees, wrote: "As the man living near was not willing to have her buried there, and as no plank could be obtained for a coffin, the corpse was carried all day in the wagon, and at night a coffin was made, and the next morning she was buried near the graves of some other Cherokees who had died in a detachment preceding us."

In November the last of the thirteen detachments, a small group led by Chief John Ross, reached Kentucky. There Ross had to leave his detachment because his wife was ill.

Ross had intended to make the overland trip with his people and enrolled with General Scott with thirty-one people, eighteen horses, and some oxen. He had hired a white contractor, Thomas Clark, to issue supplies to emigrants at Nashville. Ross asked him to find a few more horses and vehicles for his group for the trip. Clark wrote to report he "had found a good carriage and a pretty good team," at a total cost of $625. He also had found a "carryall," a light carriage for several passengers that one horse could pull.

But Clark warned Ross against trying to take his frail wife overland. He knew that roads were bad and feared that the Mississippi River might later be impassable for weeks. The unusually severe winter had frozen rivers to the north. In a few weeks ice would break up and cause problems farther down the river. Clark advised Ross to go at once by boat or find a safe place for his family until spring.

Quatie Ross was then middle-aged, the mother of five children. One writer commented that she was among the many Cherokee women "who had been as gently reared as any white woman and was no more fit for winter travel by wagon and horseback than anyone else not used to hardship. . . ."

Until 1835 Mrs. Ross had lived quietly in a comfortable house, helped by servants. For many years she had lived in fear for her husband and family because of the threats of forced removal, but she had never suffered hardships until her home was taken during her husband's absence. The hardships of the trail were beyond her experience.

Quatie Ross, wife of Chief John Ross, died near Little Rock. "This noble woman died a martyr to child-hood," Private John Burnett wrote, "giving her only blanket for the protection of a sick child." (Museum of the Cherokee Indian, Cherokee, North Carolina)

John Burnett wrote: "On the morning of November 17th we encountered a terrific sleet and snow storm with freezing temperatures and that day . . . the sufferings of the Cherokees were awful. The trail of the exiles was a trail of death. . . . They had to sleep in the wagons and on the ground without fire. And I have known as many as twenty-two . . . to die in one night of pneumonia."

Ross had wanted to travel as the other Cherokees did, but when his wife became seriously ill he decided he had to find another way. He was able to hire a boat in Paducah. The *Victoria*, a sturdy little craft, made its way safely down the Ohio and Mississippi Rivers to the Arkansas River.

Quatie Ross's condition did not improve. She died near Little Rock. Witnesses reported that she had given her only blanket to a sick child. The child recovered, but Quatie Ross developed pneumonia. Private Burnett wrote that her "uncoffined body was buried in a shallow grave . . . far from her native mountain home." Many years later a monument in her memory was placed in Mount Holly Cemetery in Little Rock by the U.S. Daughters of 1812.

The Cherokees continuing overland crossed the Ohio River at Berry's Ferry to Golconda, Illinois. An Illinois historian wrote that ferry owner John Berry received ten thousand dollars in gold from the U.S. government for transporting fourteen thousand travelers across the river. "It took the better part of fall and winter to get them across. . . . On the Kentucky side of the river . . . the hills near the shore contain the graves of many of the Indians who died in camp while waiting to make the crossing."

In Illinois

The miles the Cherokees traveled in Illinois were few compared to what lay behind them. They crossed only the southern tip of the state, from Golconda on the Ohio River to the eastern bank of the Mississippi River, a distance of less than sixty miles. But there they suffered the most deaths. The group led by B. B. Cannon, about a year earlier, had taken only eight days to get through Illinois. In 1838–1839, five detachments took eleven weeks.

Journals, letters, and oral histories described the tragedy of the Cherokees caught in Illinois by the floating ice of the Mississippi River.

Missionary Daniel Buttrick and his wife traveled with the eleventh detachment of Cherokees. The leader of this group was Richard Taylor, one of the Cherokees who had struggled hardest to resist removal. Taylor's party entered Illinois on December 15. They had been on the road since November 1, and already fifteen of their number had died.

The Reverend Buttrick expected to find only kindness and enlightenment in a nonslave state. He was shocked by the very rough language and profanity of the first Illinois settlers he met. The first evening after crossing the river Buttrick's party

This mural on a flood wall in Golconda, Illinois, commemorates the crossing of the Cherokees from Kentucky into Illinois. (photograph by A. E. Schroeder)

found the camping spot the B. B. Cannon group had used the year before and began gathering wood. They were told by a white man nearby that they would have to move on to the next place. They went on and again selected a place for a tent and started gathering wood. They were preparing tea when word came they would have to move again. The owner would not allow Cherokees to cut or burn any wood on his property. Although night was falling, the travelers—cold, tired, and hungry—had to pack up and go on again to camp on public land.

Camping was tiring at best as Buttrick described it: "in the morning taking our own bed, etc. from the little wagon in which we sleep to the large wagon which carries it—replacing the seat—getting water—cooking breakfast, putting up things, harnessing, etc. Soon we are hurried on by the wagons we accompany to the next encampment. Here we have to undo what we did in the morning—put up our tent, get wood and water, prepare supper, fix our bed, etc."

The weather made camping worse in Illinois. Buttrick wrote continually of the "piercing cold winds" they faced. The wind blew fires out, raged through the tents, and brought limbs down on campers' heads. Once rain was so heavy fires could not be built.

The missionary grieved that to make up lost time they had to travel on Sunday. Illness caused the most delays. One day the group made only six miles instead of the average ten. Then they had to remain camped for several days because two children were dying.

Buttrick and his wife also fell ill. At the time they were in a camp half a mile from water. He credited their recovery to "War Club, our able friend," who made them a healing drink of slippery elm bark.

The missionary's lowest point came on Christmas Day when his wagon axle broke. He had to remain behind the detachment and find help because the blacksmith in their group had died. There was no place to stay but with an Illinois repairman's family. The family was poor and had no suitable space for them. Worse, the man came home drunk the first night. He could not help them until he was sober. The Buttricks had to spend another day and night in a place where they were uncomfortable and unwelcome.

Back with their group on December 30, the Buttricks found more people dying in the cold and rainy weather. On New Year's Day he preached at the funeral of a young wagon driver named Ramsey. As they caught up with the other detachments, they learned of troubles members of their group and other groups had in Illinois with large claims for burial costs. The suspicious deaths of two young men were also reported.

In Union County, Illinois, however, many of the Cherokees found kindness and hospitality. Buttrick wrote that Union County's "moral character [is] much better than any we have seen in the state." Descendants of the Cherokees on the trail were to remember the kindness their ancestors found in Jones-

Anna and Winstead Davie invited the Jesse Bushyhead family
to stay in their home while they were in Jonesboro, Illinois.
(restored photographs by Geneva Davie Wiggs)

boro. In turn, descendants of pioneers living in Jonesboro during the winter of 1838–1839 have preserved many memories
of the Cherokees.

George E. Parker, a Union County historian, wrote that generations loved "to tell and retell stories of the Cherokees." A
daughter of Winstead Davie, "a merchant, landowner, and
good citizen," recalled that her father invited Chief Bushyhead
and his family to stay in their home during their delay in Jonesboro. The Bushyheads were expecting a child; Anna Davie's
fifth child had just been born in October of that year. She insisted the Bushyheads stay with them.

The daughter recalled that her father had recently purchased
one of the earliest steam engines to come to the county. The en-
gine was operated all day to run the sawmill to make trees into
plank floors for the Cherokees' tents. It was run almost every
night to grind cornmeal to feed the Indians and others in the

The Reverend Stephen Fore-
man was the leader of one of
the detachments stranded at
the Mississippi River by ice.
The Reverend Foreman and
the Reverend Jesse Bushy-
head preached the funeral
sermons for White Path and
Fly Smith at Hopkinsville,
Kentucky. (George Washing-
ton Smith Papers, Special
Collections, Special Collec-
tions/Morris Library, South-
ern Illinois University at
Carbondale)

camps. Each morning "the commanding officer" would come to her father and pay in gold for the previous day's debt.

After leaving Jonesboro, the Reverend Bushyhead led his group to the Mississippi River. They found the detachment led by Evan Jones already there. Another group led by Stephen Foreman soon arrived. Jones wrote to Chief Ross that the ice was not solid enough to cross on, but it clogged the river so that ferryboats could not move.

James Mooney, who lived among the Cherokees for many years and collected their traditions and stories, recorded memories of the dark days the travelers spent camped on the eastern side of the Mississippi River waiting to cross. "It was January. We arrived in a snow storm. There before us struggled the great Mississippi, caught in the grip of winter, running full of ice. Huge jagged blocks crashed down the current, hitting each other with mighty shocks."

Others, interviewed decades after reaching Indian Territory, remembered the ice vividly. The river was frozen solid far out from the banks. In the center were ice chunks as big as houses. As the water flowed, the ice chunks would rear on edge and crash down. The fearful noise went on day and night for weeks. The Cherokees watched with awe. How could there be such an endless flow of ice? Mooney reported that they called it "one of the earth's great wonders."

It was a wonder that caused much suffering. Winter was at its worst, with blizzard conditions that did not let up. The travelers were weakened by disease, exhaustion, and depression. They had no escape from the cold and wet. Many needed more bedding and warm clothing. Tents and covered wagons could not keep them warm and dry.

James Mooney found that over half a century had not dimmed the memories of "that halt beside the frozen river, with hundreds of sick and dying penned up in wagons or stretched upon the ground with only a blanket to keep out the January blast." Suppliers had left enough food for humans and animals to last one detachment for two or three days. Instead, five detachments came together at the river and had to stay for weeks. Weather kept them from hunting game or searching for food to buy. Hardly any healing herbs were left from home. Nobody could find more in the deep snow. Thomas Clark wrote John Ross of the destitute condition of the Cherokees in the stranded detachments, urging him to come.

Dave Crawford of Columbia, Missouri, whose ancestors walked the Trail of Tears, remembers stories told of the wait at the Mississippi River. The Cherokees had to kill and eat some of their livestock, even draft mules. They had counted on all these animals to make a new start in the West. In addition, fewer animals to carry belongings meant that more wagons and possessions had to be abandoned.

Lewis Ross finally found a day on which he could travel to St. Louis on horseback with Indian agent W. A. Lenoir. In St. Louis, Ross managed to arrange credit in his own name. He bought a strong team and wagon and loaded it with blankets, coats, and more than five hundred pairs of shoes.

From Willard Landing in Illinois the Cherokees could see the bluffs on the west side of the Mississippi, now in the Trail of Tears State Park, but they could not reach the Missouri side because of ice in the river. Many died within sight of the bluffs. (Missouri Division of Tourism)

Back at the river, Lewis Ross gave the goods out where they were most needed. He must have saved many lives, but what he brought was only a fraction of what the people needed. They died so fast they could not be buried. The Cherokees had to cover bodies with branches. The dead would have to wait for better weather for burials.

The Reverend Jesse Bushyhead later wrote that he had been detained at the Mississippi River for a month. The Cherokees finally crossed the river to Cape Girardeau County at two sites. Buttrick reported that his detachment crossed to Bainbridge near Cape Girardeau. "At this place a sand bar in the middle extends probably half across the bed of the river. . . . Therefore it is like two rivers, crossed by two ferries, that is, two sets of boats, one conveying passengers to the bar, and the other from it."

Only three wagons and a carryall crossed the first day, January 25, but the next day the Buttricks were able to cross. They had to wait some hours at the sandbar, "where the wind blew almost a gale," but they safely reached the western bank of the river on January 26. Their luggage and the wagon carrying their tent and bed had not crossed with them; but a man living near the camps took them to his home, and they spent a comfortable first night in Missouri.

Bushyhead's group and others crossed from Willard Landing in Illinois to Moccasin Springs, Missouri, on Green's Ferry. Conversion to steam ferries was only beginning in the West, and power for ferryboats on big streams usually came from horses walking on treadmills. Some treadmills were set up so the horses went in a circle; others were on an incline so the horses had to walk uphill.

Crossing the river was a very slow process. It took the Cherokees more than two weeks to get all the detachments together again to continue the journey west. Many must have thought, as the Reverend Buttrick did, of those left behind. "We have long been looking forward to this river," he wrote; "and numbers who crossed the Ohio with us have not lived to arrive at this."

Chapter 5

Crossing Missouri

Silent, ghostly figures through the lowland fog, in creaking wagons, on horseback, and afoot, they moved wearily inland as the ferry returned for the rest of their company. They filed past in bedraggled groups—an exhausted mother with a sick child lying limp in her arms, an old man racked with a cough, travel stained, eyes dulled with misery.

—Missouri Historical Review, January 1954

In 1837 the members of the detachment conducted by B. B. Cannon crossed the Mississippi River from New Hamburg Landing in Illinois to Bainbridge, Missouri, in two days, from November 12 to November 14. The Cannon party had left Tennessee with 365 persons. Cannon had recorded the deaths of three children by the time the detachment reached the Mississippi River, and another child died on November 13 while the group was crossing the river to Missouri.

The Cherokees who came over a year later had suffered many more deaths before reaching the river; but there were still thousands who had to cross the Mississippi during the harsh December and January of 1838–1839. Some crossed from New Hamburg to Bainbridge, near Cape Girardeau, as Cannon had done. Some detachments crossed south of Cape Girardeau. Marie Exler, a historian of the Trail of Tears in Missouri, wrote that the Benge detachment crossed the river from Columbus, Kentucky, to Belmont, Missouri, in Mississippi

County. "This group came north through Benton, Kelso, and Scott City to the south part of Cape Girardeau." They then turned west and south through Dutchtown and went through what is now Wappapello Wildlife Area, west of Poplar Bluff. They continued southward to Arkansas and turned west near Batesville.

A group of the Treaty Party who refused to travel with the Ross followers was led by John A. Bell. They crossed at Memphis, went west toward Little Rock, and then up the north side of the Arkansas River past Conway, Russellville, and Fort Smith. Some historians have said the Bell party tried to disrupt the Ross detachments by sending members of their group to camps to spread discontent with Chief Ross.

Most of the Ross group crossed the river on Green's Ferry, from Willard Landing in Illinois to Moccasin Springs, about ten miles north of Cape Girardeau. Stories handed down by early settlers recorded some of their experiences.

Winter came early that year, in 1838. The leaves were still on the forest trees, and the squirrels had not laid in a sufficient supply of nuts, when without warning, a blast of frigid air from the north swept the river area and overnight froze the surface of the river when only half of the Cherokee nation had crossed. . . . The ice prevented both boat and horses from moving. The horses walked round and round a turntable, winding the ropes that pulled the boat across and back. The ice prevented them from getting a footing and floating ice jammed the boat.

The cold lasted for more than a week, and the Cherokees were not prepared for the weather. "Their clothing was not adequate; they were underfed and had little shelter." An epidemic of pneumonia hit the camps. Many died on both sides of the river.

At the site where the Cherokees landed and camped, the Trail of Tears State Park preserves the area much as it was in 1838–1839. A special monument in the park commemorates one young woman who died of cold and exposure at the camp-

Mississippi River at Moccasin Springs in the Trail of Tears State Park. (photograph by Fred Lynch, Southeast Missourian, *July 4, 1976)*

ground and was buried "on a small knoll above Moccasin Springs." The white people in the area called her Princess Otahki, but family research has shown that "Otahki" was Nancy Bushyhead Walker Hildebrand. Family members believe that she was probably the sister of the Reverend Jesse Bushyhead and the wife of Lewis Hildebrand.

Marie Exler has written that this was the only marked grave in the park. According to early accounts the young woman's husband and brother put a wooden marker over her grave. It was maintained by local settlers, but about thirty or thirty-five years later the marker was burned in a fire in the woods. Neighbors then marked the grave site with a mound of rocks and an iron cross.

There is no record of the number of deaths that occurred in the camp near Moccasin Springs. Historians have recorded one birth. A daughter was born to Jesse and Eliza Bushyhead on

January 3, 1839, soon after they crossed the river. She was named Eliza Missouri Bushyhead. The baby reached the end of the trail safely and grew up to help many young people of the Cherokee Nation.

Each detachment that crossed on Green's Ferry remained camped at Moccasin Springs until all in its group had crossed. Stories told by settlers about the stay of the Cherokees were later retold by their descendants. One who spoke often of the travelers was William Sheppard, a Cape Girardeau County businessman who owned land along the Mississippi immediately south of Moccasin Springs at Sheppard's Point. He ran a wood yard for the Mississippi River steamers and kept a store. In the 1930s his granddaughter, Ada Sheppard, remembered stories he had told about the Cherokees "who came to trade and exchange coffee, which the Government furnished them and they did not use. . . ." Miss Sheppard said her grandfather praised the "honesty, courtesy, and truthfulness" of the Indians. Some of the young women "would buy finery, hats and other things, and stand before a mirror, primping."

A painting by Brother Mark Elder in the Visitor Center at the Trail of Tears State Park commemorates some of the events that are remembered in Cape Girardeau County: At Reiman's Well in Oriole, a farm family gives food and water to the Cherokees. A couple finds a Cherokee brother and sister hiding in the woods and adopts them. A mother in a carriage holds a baby who has died. A minister tries to comfort another Cherokee woman.

Once in Missouri, some of the groups reorganized and joined other detachments. One group, according to historian Ralph Killian, "decided to stop for a while. . . . They founded a village on the bluffs below St. Marys and remained twenty years, until 1859. Sensing the [approach] of the Civil War, they decided to continue their journey. In the meantime some of them had married whites and raised families. . . . That their stay here was pleasant and they were well treated became a legend passed from one generation to another."

Most of the Cherokees who crossed at Moccasin Springs or

McKendree Chapel was built in 1819. B. B. Cannon camped at the nearby William farm on his way to Jackson. (State Historical Society of Missouri, Columbia)

Bainbridge near Cape Girardeau took the route B. B. Cannon had taken the year before. It went northwesterly, through the mining area, where the French and Spanish had established villages and towns decades before. Towns meant services, places where repairs might be made and food might be bought. Southeast Missouri, sometimes called "Swampeast Missouri," had few settlements. The New Madrid earthquakes of 1811–1812 had driven early settlers away and made travel risky.

Winter 1837: Cannon Route

Cannon's record is brief, but he gives a day-to-day account of the route he traveled across Missouri in 1837. After leaving Bainbridge, he camped and rested a day at the William farm, near Old McKendree Creek. The detachment then passed though Jackson and traveled northward. On the Farmington Road they camped at the home of the "Widow Roberts" on

This sketch of Farmington was made by Charles A. Lesueur in 1826. (State Historical Society of Missouri, Columbia)

Byrd Creek, as well as at White Water Creek and Wolf Creek. On November 20 they passed through Farmington and camped at the St. Francis River. Liquor had been available in Farmington, and Cannon reported a "considerable number drunk last night." Several did not want to go on the next day, but when he left at 8 A.M., "none remained behind."

The group passed through Caledonia and the lead mines (the Courtois diggings) in Washington County. Just as Cannon thought the health of the families was improving, the weather turned very cold, and on November 24 at "Huzza Creek" (Huzzah Creek) in Crawford County, the doctor with the group, G. S. Townsend, officially asked for a stop because of the illness in many families. He later wrote to the Bureau of Indian Affairs:

I found the increasing number of cases rendered it absolutely necessary for the detachment to discontinue its march in order that I might have some chance to combat the . . . overwhelming disease that seemed to threaten the party with destruction. I accordingly addressed a note to the Conducting Agent. . . . He did not hesitate, for indeed the wagons would have been unable to have hauled the sick, as many as 60 at that time being dangerously ill.

For his part, Cannon reported he "accordingly directed the Party to remain in camp and make the best possible arrangements for the sick." Two days later he moved the group to a nearby spring and school and got permission to put as many as he could into the schoolhouse.

Four people, including two children, died during the next few days. When the group moved on, ten days later, on December 4, there was scarcely room in the wagons for the sick. The next day Cannon left two young black wagoners who were too sick to travel with a Mr. Davis. Conditions did not improve for the rest of the trip. On December 8 they "buried Nancy Big Bear's Grand child," and it rained all day. They camped at Piney, where "no fodder was to be had," and at Waynesville, where it was extremely cold.

On December 14 they halted at the James fork of the White River, and James Starr's wife gave birth to a baby during the night. The next day they stopped at the Danforth farm early in the afternoon. The reason Cannon gave for the early stop was that the wagoners were "having horses shod until late" the night before.

Two days later it snowed, and there were two deaths, "Ellege's wife and Charles Timberlake's son (Smoker)." The next day they stopped again because of illness, and Dr. Townsend sent back to Springfield for medicine. Indian agent Lenoir, traveling with the group, reported that "We went to Danford Bros. and got 96 1/2 yards of stripped calico and 50 pair of yarn stockings." It was snowing and much colder as they waited for the medicine from Springfield.

By December 26 the Cannon group had finally reached Arkansas, but they had buried three more of their number in Missouri—a man named Dreadful Waters and two children. It was the suffering of the Cannon group in Missouri that led Dr. Townsend to write to the Bureau of Indian Affairs suggesting that water routes would be more practical than the overland route the group had taken: "Near 80 days have been consumed in traveling a distance short of 800 miles," he reported. He believed that coming to Boonville by water, leaving only two hundred miles to travel overland, would save many lives. Unfortunately Dr. Townsend's advice was not taken, and a year later a much larger group was to cross Missouri on the route Cannon had taken.

Winter 1838–1839

The detachments camped at Moccasin Springs in 1838–1839 took Green's Ferry Road toward Jackson, northwest of Cape Girardeau. At the time Jackson was the larger of the two towns, described by a later Cape Girardeau newspaper as "A twenty-three year old town in 1839 . . . third largest in the state . . . considered quite a village." Cape Girardeau County had been established in 1812, and Jackson had a log courthouse, stores, saloons, hotels, boardinghouses, stills, sawmills, and other enterprises. Services of attorneys, doctors, mechanics, and other experts were available. In 1838–1839 the town of Cape Girardeau, though a few years older than Jackson, was just becoming important to the steamboat business.

The *Jackson Advertiser* reported that one group of more than nineteen hundred Cherokees passed through after landing at Moccasin Springs. No group was that large to begin with, and many deaths had occurred, so members of different groups must have united. Rich and poor were traveling together. "Some of them have considerable wealth and make a very respectable appearance," the newspaper reported; "but most of them are poor. . . ." A story in the *Jackson Advertiser,* reprinted by the *Little Rock Gazette,* reported that altogether thirteen to fourteen thousand Cherokees passed through the town.

The Cherokees still had many miles to go across Missouri in the worst part of the winter. Evan Jones, apparently one of the first to leave Cape Girardeau, wrote from Little Prairie, in what is now Phelps County, on December 30, 1838. "We have now been on our road to Arkansas seventy-five days and have traveled five hundred and twenty-nine miles. We are still nearly 300 miles short of our destination. . . . It has been exceedingly cold . . . we have, since the cold set in so severely, sent a company ahead every morning, to make fires along the road, at short intervals." Jones reported that the "thinly clad" in the group were very uncomfortable, and the fires helped.

The Richard Taylor detachment did not leave Cape Girardeau until the middle of February. The Reverend and Mrs. Buttrick stayed with different families in Cape Girardeau for three weeks after crossing the Mississippi River. Buttrick reported that about half the detachment had gotten across when the "ice began to run" and stopped the ferries again. During that time five individuals in the detachment had died—one Cherokee woman, one black man, and three Cherokee children. Twenty-six of the group had died since crossing the Tennessee River.

On February 14 Buttrick was told the detachment would move on the next day. Chief Ross had met with detachment leaders in Jonesboro, Illinois, probably because Thomas Clark had written him how much he was needed to "dispell the gloom and settle the doubts" about the emigration. "You are the master workman," Clark had written, and Ross had come to see for himself the dangerous situation of the five detachments trapped at the river. He had urged them to travel on as quickly as possible once they were across the Mississippi. As a result, the detachments were sometimes forced to travel on Sundays.

By February 22 the Taylor detachment passed through the "handsome little village of Caledonia." Buttrick was pleased by what he saw: "The village is neat and the country around delightful. The people also appear to be intelligent and well bred. Thus far we are more and more pleased with Missouri, and the very name conveys delight to our minds. We camped in a clean and pleasant place by the side of a small creek."

Dr. W. I. I. Morrow was also traveling with the Taylor detachment. He spent a few days alone in Potosi, caring for a Mr. Thompson. He described Potosi's citizens as "respectable and

Dr. W. I. I. Morrow, traveling with the Richard Taylor detachment, spent several days in Potosi in February 1839. (State Historical Society of Missouri, Columbia)

apparently pious." But he thought the town was badly laid out. "The Court house out of town, the jail burned down, two brick churches, 4 taverns, 5 or 6 good stores, some groceries and some neat dwellings made of wood & painted."

He met several interesting people and visited the smelting furnace a mile from town with a young man from Massachusetts who was trying to get an English school started. Mr. Thompson was still very ill on February 22, but Dr. Morrow paid his lodging bill and left for Caledonia to rejoin the detachment.

Rain had set in, and on February 25 Buttrick reported the death of a young Cherokee of mixed blood; he had been ill since the detachment crossed the Tennessee River some four months earlier. Two days later, during a stop near Maramec Spring it began to snow, and four more died, two from the same family.

Dr. Morrow wrote of the Massey (now Maramec) Iron Works, where he examined the forge and furnace. He was im-

Philippe Renault, the son of a wealthy French ironmaster, came to Missouri in the 1720s and discovered lead in the area of present-day Old Mines in Washington County and Mine La Motte in Madison County. The photograph shows the original Renault furnace built around 1739. (State Historical Society of Missouri, Columbia)

pressed: "I think it is the most convenient and splendid place of the kind I ever saw."

On February 28 he stopped at a Mr. Wilson's. Wilson's father-in-law, Mr. Singleton, "an eccentric old fellow—had an egg nog & stew—Mr. S. made his dog sing." Morrow was very homesick and tried "hard to get to return home, Mr. Taylor would not consent."

By March 1 four more in the detachment had died, a man and three children. March was to bring the extremes of Missouri weather that were so hard for the weary and discouraged travelers. On March 1 Buttrick wrote, "The day was beautiful, and warm as May, so that we began to talk of summer." That night, hearing thunder and what he thought was rain, he hurried outside and found summer had changed to winter: "Instead of rain we were beset with hard (round) snow. Soon, however, the snow fell in flakes, and covered the ground about ankle deep. I kindled our fire, but the wind kept whirling in almost every direction. . . . We soon found ourselves [in] a Northern winter, and could not secure ourselves from the piercing cold. I told my dear wife that it seemed almost as if we should perish." Next day after passing through woods, the Buttricks found a house and stopped, hoping to get warm. They were told by "an unseen voice" that they could not warm by the fire as the house was full.

Dr. Morrow also reported the "sudden Snow storm from the North." Mrs. Thompson, whose husband Dr. Morrow had treated in Potosi, arrived in camp and told him her husband had died. It remained cold, and Morrow complained of "a mean man" below Bates. He would not "let any person connected with the emigration stay with him."

There were good and bad days to follow. Buttrick wrote that on March 5 they traveled about "12 miles to a settlement called Port Royal on the banks of a beautiful stream called Rubedoo [Roubidoux]. Here we had a delightful place on the banks of the river, convenient to wood and water. We employed our kind Nancy, a black woman, to wash and [we] dried our clothes in the evening by the fire." Dr. Morrow also had a pleasant March 5. He "stayed at Col. Swinks—a genteel man, & pretty wife & quite *familiar.*"

In spite of pleasant days, Buttrick found it was hard to keep his spirits up. On March 9 he wrote: "We are now drawing near the Arkansas, that land of spiritual darkness, and [I] fear I am becoming more and more unfit for the holy warfare." A few days later he learned another group was catching up with the Taylor detachment. This was not welcome news to Richard Taylor.

One large group had not gone through Farmington but had traveled through Fredericktown and camped in Arcadia Valley. Writer Theodore P. Russell recalled years later that it was a very muddy February: "All the other divisions had gone by the way of Farmington, but the roads were so bad the last division had to come this way." Russell, whose family had moved from New England to the Missouri frontier the year before, was then eighteen years old. A few days before the Cherokees arrived, an agent had come to find suitable camping sites and buy feed for the teams. Only one man in the community had feed to spare. He hired Russell's father to send his son to haul oats and fodder, while his own team hauled corn.

Russell's newspaper column on the Cherokee camp is included in *A Connecticut Yankee in the Frontier Ozarks*, published by the University of Missouri Press. Even years later, he seemed to be unaware of the hardships the Cherokees had suffered; but his description of the camp provides many details about life on the trail. He thought there were about two thousand Cherokees in the group that camped on Knob Creek. The camps extended along the west bank of the creek, at the foot of Shepherd Mountain, for almost a mile. Russell noticed that as the "Indians came in they were furnished with rations by lodges, each . . . so much corn, so much oats, so much fodder." The family to arrive first took the first assigned spot, the second the next spot, and so on. It was planned that the last to arrive would be in a position to start first the next morning.

After the supplies had been distributed, the agent asked Russell if he wanted to see the camp, offering to show him "how Indians lived." The description of the camp Russell wrote later gives details the agent pointed out to him and those an eighteen year old might notice. He saw that each family group had cut a large tree. A fire was built next to it and "on the butts of the logs I saw square holes cut out that would hold about four quarts." The agent explained: "that is their grist mill; they shell some corn into the hole and take that big pounder you see there, and pound the corn until it is fine enough for bread; then they sift it and make bread of it." Russell was amazed that the women could make the meal so quickly; they soon had enough for bread for the family, or "lodge," as he called it.

As he walked through the camp, hunters came in from every direction with game. "Some used guns, but most that I saw had bows and arrows. We met one Indian with a string of fox squirrels, every one . . . had a hole through his neck made by an arrow. Some had deer, some had turkeys and smaller game."

Russell seemed most interested in the games the young people were playing: "I saw the groups of boys at different places at play. I do not know what some of their games were but some were pitching arrows, some of the larger ones shooting at a target on a tree with bow and arrows, and it is surprising how close they will shoot. I was shown how they make their bows, how they fasten the feather to the shafts of the arrow and how the points were fastened on."

Groups of girls were playing a game like badminton, and when Russell "heard the joyous laughter of the boys and girls, I could hardly realize that I was in an Indian camp, among a people that had been called *Savages* so short a time before." Like many of the early settlers along the Trail of Tears, Russell did not know the long history of the Cherokees or that many could read as well as he could. In the "Far West," as Russell's parents called Missouri, the achievements of the Cherokees in their southeastern homeland were not generally known.

If the young people Russell met resented having an outsider in camp, he did not notice. He did realize that many of the older men and women seemed "as though their hearts were full of hate toward the white race." And he noticed that the tables were set with fine dishes, "and the food looked as good and smelt as good as any white folks'!"

At some of the campsites, he wrote, the agent "called my attention to the girls dressed in silks and satins, with their ears loaded with jewelry, their hair done up in style. . . . The girls were just as handsome as any girls and had fine forms, straight as an arrow."

Arcadia Valley historians believe that the detachment Russell visited was led by Peter Hildebrand. Arcadia Valley had been home to a tribe of Delaware Indians, who lived at the foot of Pilot Knob Mountain until 1815. The area was known to the Delawares and early French and Spanish explorers as "The Lost Cove." It had been considered a famous hunting ground, and apparently game was still plentiful. The next morning as the detachment left camp, Russell reported, the hunters "spread out like a fan, and started through the woods towards the next camping place, about ten miles ahead, and swept

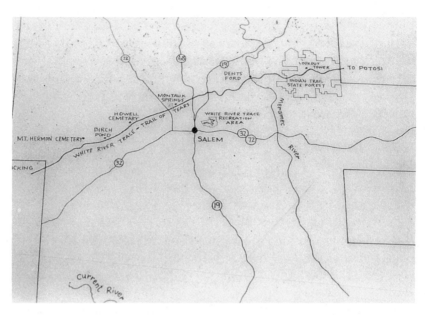

This map of the Trail of Tears in Dent County is on a marker on Missouri Route 19 north of Salem. (photograph by A. E. Schroeder)

everything before them in the way of game. During the day the deer could be seen running . . . in every direction across fields and roads."

A sign at the White River Trace Conservation Area in Dent County notes that "Peter Hildebrand's group of 1,766 Cherokees followed the Trace through Dent County and rejoined the other detachments at Marshfield." A trace is a path or trail made by the feet of people or animals. Dent County historians who have researched the history of the Trail of Tears report that the Cherokees entered the northeastern part of present-day Dent County in what is now Indian Trail State Forest. A huge white oak tree once located in the state forest was called the Indian Chief Tree. It was named for a chief who had camped under it on the Trail of Tears. The tree stood until 1890, when it was chopped down for fuel by the Sligo Furnace Company in spite of efforts to save it.

In an article about the White River Trace in the *Missouri Conservationist* of August 1992 Lori Simms wrote that the level Salem plateau provided springs, good grass for animals, wood for campfires, and many kinds of game for the traveling Cherokees.

Researchers agree that it is probably impossible to map exact trails of the Cherokee passage through the area. Numerous paths developed when groups or parts of groups struck off to take a shortcut or to rejoin others. But they believe the Hildebrand detachment crossed the Meramec River at Dent's Ford after leaving the forest. They camped at Montauk Spring, about two miles northwest of present-day Salem. Farther on, they crossed Holt Creek and buried several people at Howell Cemetery. More deaths were to come: Mount Hermon Cemetery had recently been established, and the first grave there was for a Cherokee child.

As in many areas along the trail, some residents of Dent County can trace their heritage back to a Cherokee ancestor who decided to settle there. One who stayed was Wesley Wade Watson, son of a Scottish father and a Cherokee mother. In the mid-1800s Watson and his son built several of the first gristmills in the area.

An article in the May 1995 *National Geographic* reports that Hildebrand's party of 1,766 "camped a month by Missouri's Gasconade River, too sick to travel." According to this report, cold and disease killed fifty-five members of the group there.

Diseases took their toll on all the groups moving west; among diseases reported were typhoid, measles, scarlet fever, flu, pneumonia, tuberculosis, and cholera. Cholera was one of the worst. It could cause death within twenty-four hours. Exhaustion was another serious problem: One Cherokee later recalled that his father, an old man, suddenly collapsed in the snow and could not get up. Space was made for him in a wagon, but he died the next day. A week later his mother fell and could "speak no more." Then one by one his brothers and sisters, five in all, fell ill and died. All were buried by the trail. Those left struggled on, but "while they marched their ears were filled with crying and moaning from the wagons that carried the children, the aged, the sick and the dying. The moaning through days and nights so impressed itself on [the Cherokee's] mind that he still seemed to hear it after years had passed."

The Reverend Buttrick, traveling with Richard Taylor's detachment, wrote that his group reached the "handsome river, called the Gasconade" on March 6. On March 11 Taylor received word that Hildebrand's detachment, traveling on another road, intended to reach their road five miles ahead the next day. He requested his group start before daybreak the next morning, and in this way they "took the road before Mr. Hildebrand." As the Taylor detachment approached Springfield it was again snowing and cold. On the night of March 12 there was a severe storm. The Buttricks' tent was blown over, and rain soaked them and their belongings. The rain turned to snow, and they passed through a "large prairie and arrived at Springfield, a pleasant village about noon." Morrow called Springfield "a rich country," but he was disappointed there was no letter from home waiting for him there.

The Hildebrand and Taylor detachments did not linger in the Springfield area, but reports show other groups stopped and were welcomed. O. K. Armstrong, a longtime staff writer for *Reader's Digest*, wrote a "fact-fiction" book about the Trail of Tears, assisted by his wife, Marjorie Moore Armstrong. *The Cherokee Trail* was based on research of local history. It describes a rally in Springfield for Senator Tom Benton that took place on the day that one detachment arrived. The group camped two miles south of town near a big spring. The homeowner provided two barns as bathhouses, and rocks were heated to warm the water. Armstrong also described a "dog and pony show," which had been set up on the west side of town. He wrote that some of the men from the camp went to see the ponies and dogs perform "amazing tricks" and visit the sideshows. Before the group left the camp at Springfield, four children who had died of pneumonia and a Cherokee woman were buried near the campground.

Richard Craker, a Cherokee Quapaw, who lives near Monett, has collected many stories about Indian tribes in the area, some by word of mouth. He has read that Cherokees camped on Springfield's square. Perhaps some did, but Craker thinks it more likely that they got water there and then looked for nearby Indian villages. He knows there were settlements of Cherokees, Delawares, Osages, Kickapoos, and others in the area, in spite of Missouri's efforts to move all Indian tribes out of the state.

He believes the Cherokees on the trail would have gone to their own people if possible, especially to bury the dead. Along the trail it had often been hard to get burial sites and permission for burials. Craker also believes many Cherokees may have dropped out of the march in or near Springfield. They may have stopped for a rest with relatives and friends and decided to settle. Many people of Cherokee ancestry live in the area today.

Missionaries had translated many hymns into Cherokee, and witnesses along the trail report that the Cherokees often sang hymns and their own tribal songs as they traveled. An Oklahoma writer told the story of Walini, famous for her voice, who sang all along the Trail of Tears. One song she sang was about the trail and the homeland at the end of the trail. As the travelers reached southwest Missouri, they could hope the end of the trail was near. They hoped to soon see the new homeland Walini sang of:

> "Where the bounding deer awaits us
> And the feasts are spread before us."

On March 14 the Taylor detachment traveled seventeen miles "over a barren desert . . . almost naked hills rose to view as far as the eye could reach." But they found a beautiful place to camp on a "small stream called Sugar Creek." Just before they reached the camp a heavy wagon ran over an Indian child's head. Morrow was called, and the next day Buttrick mentioned that the child was improving.

Walini, the Cherokee woman who sang along the trail. (Nineteenth Annual Report of the Bureau of American Ethnology, 1897–1898)

Morrow spent the night of March 16 "at Lock's in Barry County on Flat Creek, a branch of White River. Lock a gambler and hunter. Did not sleep much. The boys and girls talked and laughed all night." The Buttricks drove ahead the next day and spent their last two days in Missouri with a Mr. Mason. "Our host was from Tennessee—has a pleasant family and good accommodations for travelers."

On March 18 the detachment crossed into Arkansas from Missouri "near Meeks on Sugar Creek 7 miles northeast of Pratt," according to Morrow. Buttrick reported the day was windy and dusty, but later in the evening a thunderstorm brought heavy rain.

The routes of the Trail of Tears across Missouri have not been completely traced by local historians and the National Park Service. We do know that after leaving Cape Girardeau and

Jackson, traveling Cherokees passed through or near these Missouri towns: Greenville, Fredericktown, Farmington, Caledonia, Poplar Bluff, Cabool, Steelville, St. James, Jerome, Waynesville, Oakland, Conway, Marshfield, Springfield, Crane, Cassville, and Washburn. Some of the towns did not exist at the time; some no longer exist or now have new names.

The trail went through or into the present-day counties of Cape Girardeau, Perry, Bollinger, Madison, St. Francois, Washington, Crawford, Dent, Phelps, Pulaski, Laclede, Webster, Greene, Christian, Stone, and Barry.

With such large numbers of travelers it was necessary for different groups or parts of groups to take different routes. A new route would offer more game and local supplies and more animals for sale or barter.

The Cherokees took some good memories from Missouri. Dave Crawford says his grandparents told him of a community somewhere in Missouri that opened its church to shelter the travelers. People also brought some cattle and slaughtered them for the Cherokees to eat. There were memories of "poor broken country" and "narrow rich bottoms," of "warm pleasant days" and "snow storms from the North," of kind people and others not so kind.

Wherever the Cherokees passed in Missouri, local historians are working to collect and preserve their story. The Trail of Tears across Missouri has not been forgotten by descendants of those who witnessed it.

Chapter 6

Arkansas and Beyond

Dec. 26th: Halted [at] Cane Hill, Ark.

Dec. 27th: Buried Alsey Timberlake, Daughter of Chas. Timberlake. Marched at 8 A.M.

Dec. 28th: Buried another child of Chas. Timberlake and one that was born (untimely) yesterday.

—Journal of B. B. Cannon

The party led by B. B. Cannon was in Arkansas, on the "right hand road to Cane Hill," on December 25. On December 28 they refused to go farther. But they promised Cannon they would stay together until an officer arrived from Fort Gibson. The officer arrived, and on December 30 Cannon checked the rolls and turned the group over to the army. The detachment had been traveling for seventy-seven days. Fifteen members of the group had died. Charles Timberlake had lost three children in the last few days of travel.

The detachment led by John Benge, which had turned south from Missouri, passed Smithville, Arkansas, in Lawrence County on December 13, 1838. The *Arkansas Gazette* of January 2 printed a report on the detachment sent by a local resident.

About twelve hundred Indians passed through. . . . The whole company appears to be well clothed, and comfortably fixed for traveling. I am informed that they are very peaceable. . . . They have upwards of one hundred wagons; . . . their horses are the finest I have seen in such a collection. The company consumes about one hundred and fifty bushels of corn a day.

It is stated that they have the measles and the whooping cough among them, and there is an average of four deaths a day.

Two days later the detachment passed near Batesville. An article in the *Batesville News* of December 20 reported that many of the travelers had visited Batesville to get "carriages repaired, horses shod, etc." A local minister wrote that Cherokee leaders George Lowrey and William S. Coodey and a Dr. W. P. Rawles of Gallatin, Tennessee, were traveling with the group. The minister had served as a missionary to the Cherokees and wrote of the good character of the Cherokee people he had known.

The Cherokee detachments that took the Cannon route in Missouri crossed the northwestern corner of Arkansas, through Benton and Washington Counties. Cane Hill, where Cannon had camped, had been established in 1827. Historians report that the first settlers there led packhorses over buffalo trails too narrow for wagons. By 1835 Presbyterians had opened an academy in Cane Hill in a two-room log cabin.

For the Buttricks their first night in Arkansas brought more rain: "We had just composed ourselves to sleep in our little Carry all when we were awakened by loud peals of thunder and a heavy rain falling upon us. One shower followed another so that we had but little sleep." It was not until almost a week later that the detachment reached its destination, "the place of deposit . . . where Mr. Taylor is to deliver the detachment over to the . . . officers who are to supply . . . provisions [for] one year."

Arkansas historians report that eleven detachments of Cherokees crossed northwest Arkansas. Some of the groups entered the state at Gateway, south of Seligman, Missouri. They crossed what is today Pea Ridge National Military Park and went on toward Maysville. The route closely followed what are today Arkansas Route 72 and a small section of U.S. Route 62.

Arkansas had just become a state in 1836, and the town of Bentonville, named for Missouri Senator Tom Benton, was only a year old. Fayetteville, founded in 1828, was the largest town in the area.

Early Ozarks settlers who saw the Cherokees passing by would have seen some people warmly dressed, others barefoot, their shoes long ago worn out. Many who had left home with much valuable property had become poor on the trip. Belongings had been lost in river crossings or to vandals who preyed on the travelers. Possessions had been traded to pay tolls for crossing landowners' property when money was exhausted. Often when an animal or vehicle broke down there was no choice but to abandon it. Burying their dead along the trail was sometimes a privilege for which Cherokees had to pay.

To begin with, observers reported, Cherokees drove everything from the roughest farm wagon to the most stylish light carriage. But at best the fine harness horses some started out with would have been badly failing by the end of the long trip. At worst they would have died along the way, and owners might not have been able to replace them. The same would be true for draft horses, mules, and oxen. Their work at home would not have conditioned them for such a trip.

Arkansas settlers would no doubt have viewed the Cherokees as other observers had viewed them along the way. In November of 1837 the *Arkansas Gazette* had complained that the "vast . . . efforts made by the general government to rid the interior of our Union of the presence of its Indian tribes, have made our State for the present, nothing but a thoroughfare for the march of these tribes to their new homes in the west." Some observers would have realized the hardships the Cherokees had endured to reach Arkansas. To others they may have represented disease and a possible threat to the area, so their quick departure was much desired.

Nobody could have guessed the importance Arkansas would have in future Cherokee history. Within a few months a famous Cherokee would die there, and other Cherokees would be returning to the state for refuge. In less than three decades

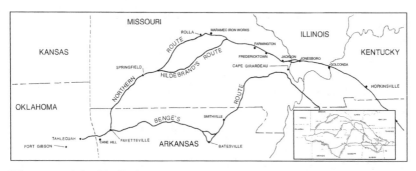

The map of the Trail of Tears shows the route taken by many of the detachments moving from Tennessee to their new home in the West. (adapted by Donald M. Lance from Comprehensive Management and Use Plan*)*

Cherokees would fight and die for the Confederacy at the Battle of Pea Ridge.

If Walini's song reflected their expectations, "feasts are spread before us," the Cherokees soon met sad disillusion in the Indian Territory. The detachments arrived in the territory from early January to late March 1839. Elijah Hicks, with a party of 856, arrived on January 4. On January 17 the group of 1,103 led by John Benge arrived. The Reverend Evan Jones brought his group in on February 2, and the Reverend Jesse Bushyhead arrived on February 23. The Reverend Stephen Foreman arrived on February 27. Last to arrive were the detachments led by Richard Taylor and Peter Hildebrand: Taylor on March 24 and Hildebrand on March 25. The Bushyhead detachment had traveled 178 days, Taylor's detachment 185 days, and Hildebrand's 154 days.

No generous supplies of food awaited them, no farming equipment, none of the promised payment for possessions left in the Southeast. Instead, there was only more of the inferior, sometimes useless, rations they had received on the trail. John Ross bought them necessary food, using the last of the funds for travel he had received before they set forth. The contract with the government had been based on an estimate of eighty days of travel, with the understanding that additional pay would be provided for additional time. But President Van Buren turned down Ross's claim for additional funds. The claim was not paid until September 6, 1841.

The Cherokees found little, if any, warm welcome from emigrants who had gone before them. There were three separate factions now together in the West: the Old Settlers were those who had been moving west since the 1700s; the members of the Treaty Party, those who had signed the Treaty of New Echota; and the majority, those who had given their support to Chief Ross.

The resentment felt toward the Treaty Party by those who had traveled the Trail of Tears was deep and bitter. Before the Taylor detachment had left for the West, a group had gathered at one of the tents and adopted three resolutions: "that while on the road they would spend the Sabbath in the worship of God," as far as it was possible; that they would "regard their spiritual interests in selecting plans to settle in the West"; and that they "would not unite in Christian fellowship with those who had made, signed or executed the New Echota Treaty, without a confession on their part." The suffering they had endured on the way west had only deepened their resolve.

Those who had been longest in Indian Territory had, of course, settled on the best land. Few were secure enough to see the newcomers as anything but competitors in a life-and-death struggle. The Old Settlers had their own chiefs and laws and were not interested in uniting with the Ross Cherokees. Some openly resented them.

After a dispirited stay in a camp, in which thousands waited, the Cherokees gave up their hope that the government would fulfill its promises. They drifted off to find places to live. The 7 million acres set aside for the Cherokees sounds generous, but much of the land was unfit for cultivation, and more was marginal. It was entirely different from the land Cherokees knew how to farm, and the seasons were different. Everyone had to learn through hunger what worked and what did not work with the new soil and the new climate.

For some time the Cherokee emigrants had to go back to almost forgotten old ways of doing things. Elders taught younger people how to hunt and trap and make shoes and clothing from animal hides. Previously pampered children learned to do hard, menial work.

Families who had animals or tools shared with those who had none. People who had nothing else to give contributed their labor. They helped each other build homes and work fields. But crops and equipment often failed. Many people and animals, weakened by the Trail of Tears, died. There was almost no medical help available, though the two or three missionaries who had been trained to aid doctors helped as best they could.

It was a bitterly discouraging time, and one of the most disappointing aspects for some of the Ross supporters was seeing the Ridges comfortably set up. Members of the wealthy family already had built homes. Some had big farms and slaves to work them. Their large store stood ready to serve everyone's needs. In *Cherokee Tragedy,* a book sympathetic to the Ridge family, author Thurman Wilkins reports that they had taken great trouble and expense to stock the store. They offered generous credit terms to tribe members. Sales on account soon rose to ten thousand dollars, a huge amount for the time.

The Ridges had decided they wanted no more part in tribal business. They would just farm and keep their store. But this was not enough to buy the good will they had hoped to gain. Cherokees loyal to Ross saw the Ridges as traitors. They felt the family had saved its fortune at the tribe's expense. The Ridges had broken the rule against selling tribal land. Revenge was inevitable. It came from within a group of volunteers, executioners selected by old tribal custom.

Major Ridge died first, early on June 22, 1839, in Arkansas. He had made an overnight stop en route to Van Buren to visit a sick slave, and he was crossing White Rock Creek a few miles from Cane Hill with one servant boy. The two had stopped to let their horses drink.

Suddenly, from ambush, came a burst of shots. Twelve bul-

John Ridge. The son of Major Ridge met Sarah Bird Northrup, his white wife, while he was at the Foreign Mission School in Cornwall, Connecticut. (Museum of the Cherokee Indian, Cherokee, North Carolina)

lets from several guns hit Major Ridge, and he slid into the water. His panicked young horse trampled him. Marks its new shoes made could be seen in the sandstone stream bank for many years.

As Major Ridge died, his cherished son John lay bleeding to death in his home at Honey Creek in Indian Territory. He had been dragged from his bed and stabbed twenty-five times. Then he was walked on before the eyes of his children, a Cherokee gesture of contempt. One writer noted that the murderers of John Ridge probably wore clothing from his family's store that was bought on credit. John's wife, despite her grief, sent a runner to try to find her father-in-law and warn him, but it was too late.

Elias Boudinot, Major Ridge's nephew, the man who had developed and edited the *Cherokee Phoenix*, was killed on the same day. He was approached at the mission by two tribesmen requesting medicine for their families. Dispensing medi-

Elias Boudinot was a cousin to John Ridge and the brother of Stand Watie. He was the first editor of the Cherokee Phoenix. *(Museum of the Cherokee Indian, Cherokee, North Carolina)*

cine was one of Boudinot's duties. As he turned to go to the store to get it, he was attacked from behind with a knife and a hatchet.

At the time of his death, Boudinot and missionary Samuel Worcester were working on a translation of the Bible into Cherokee. Boudinot was in sight of Worcester's house when he was killed, and the attack was seen by others.

Boudinot's brother, Stand Watie, was also a target, but Worcester sent a boy to the Ridge store to warn him. After what seemed a casual conversation over the sugar barrel, the boy went looking around the store. Watie left by a back door and jumped on the horse Worcester had sent. Comet, the fastest horse the missionary owned, took Watie to safety. He was to remain a problem to John Ross for the rest of the chief's life.

The assassination of the Ridges threw the Cherokees into turmoil and feuding. Several more people died. John Ross was never connected with the deaths, but his supporters feared for his life. As James Mooney wrote, "there can be no question that the men were killed in accordance with the law of the Nation." The death Major Ridge had expected when he signed the Treaty at New Echota had come to three leaders of the Treaty Party.

At this time of trouble the Cherokee people showed their loyalty to Ross. Hundreds of them came and camped around his home. They wanted to protect him from harm. A killer would have to go through them to get to their chief.

John Ridge's wife took their children into Arkansas and never brought them back. They settled in the Little Rock area, and she made sure that the children were educated as their father and grandfather would have wished. Sarah Bird Ridge, a white woman, had met her husband when he was attending school in Connecticut, but she did not go back to her birth family. She stayed close to the tribe so her children could know their father's relatives.

Major Ridge's aging wife fled with her daughter-in-law. A number of other relatives and supporters also left, fearing more executions. The older Mrs. Ridge eventually returned to the nation and resumed work in the family store. Many Ridge loyalists never returned.

Chapter 7

Founding a New Home

We, the old settlers, are here in council with the late emigrants, and we want you to come up without delay, that we may talk matters over like friends and brothers. These people are here in great multitudes, and they are perfectly friendly towards us. They have said, over and over again, that they will be glad to see you, and we have full confidence they will receive you in friendship.
—Lines to the western chiefs by Sequoyah

During the spring and summer of 1839 John Ross worked to try to unify the eastern and western Cherokees under one government. The assassination of the Ridges and Boudinot caused continuing unrest, but on September 6, 1839, a new constitution, based on the old one, was formally adopted by the council representing both groups. The Reverend Jesse Bushyhead and Sequoyah had helped to bring the groups together. John Ross was elected principal chief.

Feuding between the two groups continued, however, and President Van Buren refused to recognize Ross. In February 1840 some members of the Old Settlers and the Treaty Party held a meeting at Fort Gibson and adopted a resolution against Ross and his followers. But a U.S. House of Representatives committee sided with the Ross party, charging President Van Buren and the War Department with unjustified interference in the affairs of the Cherokees.

In 1841 President John Tyler assured the Ross majority of

Cherokee Syllabary

a	e	i	o	u	v
D a	R e	T i	Ꭷ o	O u	i v
Ꭶ ga Ꮖ ka	Ꮁ ge	Ꮿ gi	A go	J gu	E gv
Ꮧ ha	Ꮄ he	Ꮽ hi	F ho	Ꮁ hu	Ꮣ hv
W la	Ꮧ le	Ꮅ li	Ꮉ lo	M lu	Ꮃ lv
Ꮵ ma	Ꭰ me	H mi	Ꮉ mo	Ꮍ mu	
Ꮎ na Ꮤ hna Ꮉ nah	Ꮑ ne	Ꮒ ni	Ꮓ no	Ꮔ nu	Ꮒ nv
Ꮖ qua	Ꮙ que	Ꮗ qui	Ꮖ quo	Ꮛ quu	Ꮝ quv
Ꮔ sa Ꭴ s	Ꮞ se	Ꮢ si	Ꮪ so	Ꮟ su	Ꮢ sv
Ꮮ da Ꮤ ta	Ꮥ de Ꮦ te	Ꮧ di Ꮨ ti	V do	S du	Ꮃ dv
Ꮪ dla Ꮭ tla	Ꮭ tle	Ꮳ tli	Ꮻ tlo	Ꮬ tlu	P tlv
Ꮝ tsa	Ꮴ tse	Ꮵ tsi	K tso	Ꮦ tsu	Ꮳ tsv
Ꭼ wa	Ꮺ we	Ꮻ wi	Ꮼ wo	Ꮽ wu	6 wv
Ꮿ ya	Ᏸ ye	Ᏹ yi	Ꮂ yo	Ᏻ yu	B yv

Ꮳ Ꮃ Ꭹ   tsa la gi   *Cherokee*

Ꮢ Ꮹ Ꮿ   si quo ya   *Sequoyah*

The Cherokee syllabary developed by Sequoyah. (courtesy Donald M. Lance)

support, but trouble between the groups continued. Some of the Old Settlers and members of the Treaty Party emigrated to Texas; some appealed to Washington for a division of the tribe. After an investigation, the government again sided with the majority. Representatives of the government finally signed a treaty on August 6, 1846, agreeing that the lands in the Cherokee Nation were for all Cherokees. Officials promised to reimburse the nation for sums owed for years for lands and possessions in the East. Witnesses at the meeting reported that after the treaty was signed John Ross and Stand Watie shook hands.

Gradually the Cherokees remaining in the nation achieved unity. The next years saw rapid progress, as agriculture was developed on both small farms and large plantations. Businesses thrived, schools were developed, and many Cherokees

Stand Watie became a brigadier general in the Civil War and was the last Confederate officer to surrender. He held out two months longer than General Robert E. Lee. (Archives and Manuscripts Division of the Oklahoma Historical Society)

became well-off again. Sequoyah's syllabary made it possible for young and old to learn to read.

But both unity and progress were threatened by the Civil War. John Ross wanted the tribe to remain neutral. He may have been sure the North would win. He might have felt too bitter against the South to want to fight for the Confederacy. He may have felt that the tribe could not bear the expense and stress of war. And, of course, the Cherokees had long ago agreed never to fight whites again.

Letters Ross wrote at the time show he wanted his people saved from more suffering and losses. But in 1861, in his annual message, he conceded that it seemed as if the Confederacy would win, and the tribe's best interests might lie in aligning with the South. A regiment of mounted Cherokees had already been raised, funded by the tribe, and put in the service of General Benjamin McCulloch.

Stand Watie had strongly favored joining the Confederacy, and from the beginning most young Cherokee men agreed with him that they should fight for the South. Possibly in the hope of preventing a tribal rift, Ross had not debated the issue much. To him, unity was more important. He sent his second wife, Mary, back to her family in the East for her safety.

The lovely Ross home, Rose Cottage, was destroyed in the fighting. Watie and his Confederate forces drove the Reverend Evan Jones, a strong Unionist, out of the nation. Just as Ross had feared, the tribe lost most of what it had gained—countless homes and businesses as well as seven thousand lives.

There was much to lose by then. *After the Trail of Tears,* by William G. McLoughlin, described the nation's two best towns, Tahlequah and Park Hill, in Oklahoma. Tahlequah, the largest, and the capital, had about sixteen hundred residents. It contained the tribal legislative buildings, a post office, the office of the nation's newspaper, the *Cherokee Advocate,* a dentist and attorneys, eight stores, five hotels, and many shops to supply services and merchandise. Since 1849 Tahlequah had boasted a brick Masonic temple, to which all leading members of the nation belonged.

At nearby Park Hill the wealthiest and most prominent Cherokees had their elaborate homes. The mission schools were at Park Hill, as was the Sequoyan press, which missionary Worcester kept busy producing educational and religious materials for the nation. Two large seminaries the Cherokees had built for their own young people, impressive pillared buildings, were just outside Park Hill. McLoughlin called this town "the social and intellectual center of the Nation," a place of "grace and beauty." Visitors left it deeply respectful of what the Cherokees had accomplished.

Like others in the defeated South, the Cherokees would have to start over again. Near the end of the Civil War, when the outcome was almost certain, Ross went to Washington to plead the Cherokee cause with Abraham Lincoln. He was afraid that he and his people would be punished for supporting the South. Lincoln had always been sympathetic about the

Cherokee Female Seminary at Park Hill, near Tahlequah, Oklahoma.
(Archives and Manuscripts Division of the Oklahoma Historical
Society)

hardships of the removal. He also realized the need for unity.
He excused the Cherokees for backing the Southerners.

Ross died in 1866 in Washington, D.C., still working for his
tribe. His body was brought back to the Cherokee Nation for
burial. Other principal chiefs and leaders replaced him
through the years. They guided the Cherokees through many
problems to a position of stability and power among other
tribes.

Eliza Missouri Bushyhead: A New Generation

One of the Cherokees to contribute greatly to the progress
of the Cherokee people after the Civil War was Eliza Missouri
Bushyhead. Born on the west bank of the Mississippi River in
Cape Girardeau County on January 3, 1839, Eliza grew up in

Eliza Missouri Bushy-head was born on January 3, 1839, near Moccasin Springs, Missouri. (Archives and Manu-scripts Division of the Oklahoma Historical Society)

the Cherokee Nation. Her father, the Reverend Jesse Bushy-head, settled at the Cherokee Baptist Mission, established by the Reverend Evan Jones. The site became known as "Bread-town" because it was one of the places where rations were is-sued to the emigrants. The Reverend Bushyhead was known as "one of the ablest and most successful of the native preach-ers of the Baptist church. . . . He enjoyed unequaled honor among his people."

Bushyhead died in 1844, only five years after arriving in the West, leaving nine children. The family continued to live at the Cherokee Baptist Mission, which became the center of educa-tion and Christian teaching. The second printing press in the nation was set up at the mission and in 1844 printed the first issue of the *Cherokee Messenger.*

Eliza attended the Cherokee Baptist Mission and the Chero-kee Female Seminary in Tahlequah. In 1858, while teaching school, she met and married David Rowe Vann. Vann died in 1870, and three years later Eliza married Bluford West Alberty.

The Albertys were made stewards of the Cherokee Male Seminary in Tahlequah, and Eliza became famous for her efforts to help young people. She tried to see that no boy was ever turned away from the seminary. Some way was always found to pay expenses for those who could not pay.

"Aunt Eliza," as she soon became known, was active in the political affairs of the Cherokee Nation and worked to preserve Cherokee history and relics. The Albertys bought the Cherokee National Hotel in 1885. Many prominent members of the nation and well-known U.S. officials stayed there. Her interest in young people continued, and she often took in homesick youngsters for a free meal or an overnight stay.

The Albertys' only child, a daughter, died in infancy. But Eliza raised and educated several of her nieces and nephews and adopted a full-blooded Cherokee girl. Maggie, the adopted daughter, became a teacher and married a member of the Zuni tribe. Her visits home with her children always created great interest among the Cherokees.

Eliza Alberty was widely known and well loved throughout northeastern Oklahoma. When she died on November 6, 1919, the Tahlequah paper called her "Tahlequah's most distinguished citizen." She had served her people well.

Chapter 8

Preserving Cherokee History

There is change indeed in dress and seeming, but the heart of the Indian is still his own.

—James Mooney, "Myths of the Cherokee"

Many Cherokees adopted European ways, beginning in the 1700s, but tribal members still kept the old Cherokee traditions alive. As historian Glen Lashey has observed, the story of the Cherokees resembles the story of the phoenix for which they had named their first newspaper. In the Egyptian myth, the phoenix emerges from the ashes of the fire to live another five hundred years. Lashey recalls a Cherokee saying: "The old ways are swift birds—they fly away or die and leave no sign." But today Cherokees are preserving their old ways.

Anthropologist James Mooney wrote that he lived among the Cherokees to study their traditions "in successive field seasons from 1887 to 1890." In "Myths of the Cherokee," published in the *Nineteenth Annual Report of the Bureau of American Ethnology* in 1900, Mooney traced the history of the tribe and recorded many of their traditions and traditional stories. He wrote about Swimmer and other leading medicine men, about the sacred formulas, myths, secular songs and dances, and many other very personal and sacred topics. *The Swimmer Manuscript: Cherokee Sacred Formulas and Medicinal Prescriptions,* which Mooney had taken to Washington, was published by the Bureau of American Ethnology in 1932. It recorded

Swimmer, a Cherokee medicine man. (Nineteenth Annual Report of the Bureau of American Ethnology)

many Cherokee beliefs about disease and health and described the practices of several medicine men and the few medicine women he found.

Mooney observed that the medicine men and women were the greatest supporters of the old "faith, lore, and custom" at the time he lived among them. Today many Cherokees are committed to keeping the old ways alive. The Cherokee language is taught in their homes and in elementary schools. Music, dance, and arts and crafts are handed down. Native foods are still commonly eaten in Cherokee homes.

The 1990 census showed more than 369,000 Cherokees living in the United States. Approximately 9,000 Cherokees still live on lands in North Carolina known as the Qualla Boundary. The Eastern Band of Cherokee Indians are descendants of those tribal members who escaped the removal "roundup" in 1838 by hiding in hills and caves—or those who decided to return home. In 1889 their rights were established by the North

The seal of the Cherokee Nation was adopted by act of the Cherokee National Council and approved in 1871. It symbolizes the early government structure and the endurance of the Cherokees. The seven-pointed star symbolizes the seven age-old clans of the Cherokees. (courtesy of the Cherokee Nation)

Carolina legislature, and the Eastern Band of Cherokees was formed. Over the years they have developed schools, churches, and businesses. In Cherokee, North Carolina, the Museum of the Cherokee Indian, the Oconaluftee Indian Village, and the outdoor drama "Unto These Hills" tell the story of the Cherokee people.

The Cherokee Nation of Oklahoma serves approximately 85,000 tribal members in fourteen counties in the northeastern part of the state. Tahlequah, Oklahoma, has been the capital of the Cherokees in the West since 1839. The Cherokee Heritage Center near Tahlequah includes a museum, the Rural Museum Village, and the Trail of Tears Memorial Prayer Chapel. A pageant in an outdoor amphitheater traces the story of the Cherokees in the West from the Trail of Tears to Oklahoma statehood in 1907.

Both the Eastern Band of Cherokees and the Cherokee Nation of Oklahoma have tribal governments. Their chiefs and council members are elected. Both groups carry out many educational programs for their own people and for others.

James Mooney, an anthro-pologist who lived among the Cherokees from 1887 to 1890. (Bulletin #99, Bureau of American Ethnology, The Swimmer Manuscript: Cherokee Sacred Formulas and Medicinal Prescriptions*)*

Cherokees in Missouri

A study of the 1990 census shows over 10,000 Cherokees living in Missouri. Most reported only that they were Cherokee, but some specified Eastern, Echota, Western, or Northern Cherokee.

James Mooney wrote of the legend of the "Lost Cherokee."

"When the first lands were sold by Cherokees, in 1721, a part of the tribe bitterly opposed the sale, saying . . . the whites would never be satisfied, but would soon want a little more, and a little more again, until there would be little left for the Indians. Finding [they could not] prevent the treaty, they determined to leave their old homes forever and go far into the West, beyond the great River, where the white man could never follow them."

Many Cherokees were already living west of the Mississippi River in 1838–1839. Other members of the tribe stayed in Missouri on the way west. Today, Beverly Baker-Northup of Co-

The seal of the Northern Cherokee Nation. (courtesy of the Northern Cherokee Nation of the Old Louisiana Territory)

lumbia is principal chief of the Northern Cherokee Nation of the Old Louisiana Territory. Most of her time is spent working for the Northern Cherokees. In several interviews with the author she talked about her work and her own connection to Cherokee history. She is prepared for certain questions.

People ask, "How can a woman be an Indian chief? Where are the Indians you lead? What's an Indian chief doing in Missouri?"

And when those questions are answered, two more usually follow: "How do Indian people feel about us? What do they want, really?"

She answers the questions in order.

How can a woman be an Indian Chief? "Cherokee women have always been liberated . . . always held positions of leadership. For many years a woman was chief of the country's largest group of Cherokees, those in Oklahoma. It was common, hundreds of years ago, for the wife of a fallen chieftain to assume his responsibilities. Each group of Cherokees had one or more older women whose opinion was sought and respected. Women had their places in council."

Baker-Northup explains that Cherokees are matrilineal. This means that a woman and her family have more responsibility and control over her children than the children's father and his family have. It was a logical arrangement in days when American Indian men were away hunting or often in danger of being killed. A Cherokee woman could be free of an unwanted husband simply by putting his belongings outside the door. He went his way; home and children were hers.

One of Baker-Northup's ancestors was a subchief under John Ross and walked the Trail of Tears. Nowadays, she says, chieftainships usually go to whoever will undertake the responsibility. The fact that her ancestors had been leaders was one reason she was asked to take leadership. It is also one reason she accepted the responsibility.

The biggest part of Baker-Northup's work is helping people with Indian blood who want to trace their ancestry and enroll with a tribe. This requires a lot of letter writing and almost daily interviews, by telephone or in person.

She makes frequent speaking appearances. Her listeners range from Cub Scouts and senior citizens to civic, legislative, and religious groups. She also works to seek government attention for her people.

In carrying out her duties, Baker-Northup has done extensive historical research. Getting official government recognition depends on proving that the Northern Cherokees do exist and did exist in Missouri and Arkansas before the Trail of Tears. Some ancestors of the Northern Cherokees settled west of the Mississippi River in French or Spanish Territory long before the Louisiana Purchase. They were joined by others who left for the West during the first decades of the 1800s. These groups of Cherokees already living in southeast Missouri offered refuge to those on the Trail of Tears who were too ill or too weary to continue.

It was fairly easy for Cherokees to blend into white settlements, because many of them did not look "Indian." A tribal tradition was to marry for love, with little prejudice about race or nationality. Thus many Cherokees could pass for white, or black, or a vague mix of ancestry. Early intermarriage with Scottish soldiers had resulted in many red-haired Cherokees.

Other reasons Cherokees blended easily were that many were Christian. Most dressed as the whites did. They possessed useful skills and crafts. Their success at blending has been so great that Baker-Northup says she is often asked, "Where have you Indians been all this time?"

"We have been right here among you," is her answer, "raising our children and working at our jobs." Until recently, however, few made their ancestry known, as most people of Indian blood now do. Earlier, Indian people kept low profiles in fear that the government would somehow, sometime, descend and pack them off to reservations. Elders, usually familiar with prejudice and harassment, wanted to spare their children pain. They concealed their family history.

This attitude, lingering in many older Cherokees today, is sometimes an obstacle to younger ones who want to explore their heritage. Grandparents often refuse to share what they know. "Maybe they are still afraid," Baker-Northup says. In Missouri, beginning in 1824, a series of laws made it unlawful to trade with Indians. The 1824 law specifically mentioned the "Indians settled . . . on the waters of the St. Francis river," where Cherokees had settled in the 1700s. As late as 1906 it was unlawful for any Indian to hunt or "roam" within the limits of Missouri without a "written permit from the proper agent." This law made it the duty of the governor to send a request to the agents of all the Indian tribes on the borders of the state, asking them *not* to grant a permit to "any Indian to come into the state for the purpose of hunting." The laws relating to Indians were repealed in 1909, but it made sense for the Cherokees to blend into the white communities in the early 1900s.

Baker-Northup says the hardest question she has to answer is about Indian feelings for whites. This seldom comes from audiences who have not met her before, but often, cautiously, on closer acquaintance, from individuals.

"Most of us look white, and we love our white ancestors. It's not a matter of rejecting everything white, though I must admit wishing I had more Indian blood. But the mixture naturally creates conflicts, especially as we mature.

"So much that is believed about us is untrue. . . . Even today, some advertising promotes false impressions and is offensive to anyone descended from Native Americans. For instance, some advertisements have used broken English and grunting."

Some holidays, too, create conflict. Columbus Day discussions of the European "discovery" of a new world offend those who know the long history of the American Indian. Baker-Northup is happy to see newspapers and schools starting to look at the holiday with more respect for those who were already here when Columbus came.

She agrees with the suggestion that October 12 be designated American Indian Day. She points out what a dramatic holiday that could be, with exhibitions from the varied tribal cultures. Everyone could enjoy seeing authentic Native American clothing, sampling Native American foods, and watching and participating in traditional music and dance. Colorful and interesting all-Indian parades would surely be enjoyed anywhere in the country.

As to what Indian people want, Baker-Northup will speak only for her own people. The Northern Cherokee Nation of the Old Louisiana Territory is working for national rerecognition of the tribe's existence as the sovereign nation it was to the Spanish government officials in New Orleans in the late 1700s. After the American Revolution, the Spanish granted Cherokees permission to cross the Mississippi River and settle in Spanish Louisiana. In the early 1800s, the U.S. government recognized the Cherokees west of the Mississippi River by assigning Indian agent Samuel Treat to them, according to Baker-Northup. Today, the Northern Cherokees want visibility and rerecognition of the needs of their people. The biggest problem in achieving this has been official surprise, even at the local level, at being asked for help.

"They didn't know what to do with us," Baker-Northup

smiles. "They didn't even know they had us, so few funds or procedures, if any, have been developed for our needs. There are no resources channeled our way."

Her work has taken time and many visits to Jefferson City and, in the past few years, to Washington, D.C. She has seen attitudes change. In 1983 Governor Christopher Bond issued a proclamation recognizing the Northern Cherokee "tribe, its people, and the contributions they have made to their home state." In 1984 the Missouri House of Representatives approved a resolution honoring the Cherokees who "chose Missouri as their new home."

When asked "what we want," Baker-Northup says, "beyond state and federal recognition, I can only say what I want. That is for all Indian people to unite in actively preserving our heritage. Many, nowadays, are going so far as to urge the young to marry only others of Indian descent, to strengthen the blood and prevent our becoming extinct. The world needs us."

And why is that? What would she most like to say to those who share the white part of her own heritage?

"I would just like to ask everyone to listen to us, to look at our history, to see what we are trying to share through our culture centers. There is so much in the Indian way that can help us all . . . maybe *save* us all. There are religious differences among the tribes, but all know the importance of the earth. All feel brotherhood with every other kind of life. All understand that nature was perfectly balanced, that everything was here for a purpose. But humankind has been destroying the earth and other life before finding out what our Creator intended for us. It all could still be saved. It *has* to be saved, so we, ourselves, can survive."

Although Baker-Northup is strongly committed to Christianity, she finds a lot to like in most tribal religions. They tend to center on trying to achieve inner harmony and harmony with others and with the natural world; they advocate practicing kindness and generosity, taking responsibility for others, and being unselfish, contributing members of the group. She "would like to encourage others to see the beauty in living things which our Creator has given to us. And to realize the importance of our taking care of all life."

When she speaks of such things, Beverly Baker-Northup's words take on some of the ring we associate with Native American oratory. They could have been delivered by a stately white-haired chieftain but also sound right coming from a small woman in frilly shirt and blue jeans, who sits among her plants and pets, among family pictures. She is Beverly Baker-Northup, lover of family, church, and nature—a mother, grandmother, preacher's wife, and Cherokee chief.

Chapter 9

Commemorating the Trail of Tears

It touches me deeply that people who had no ancestors on the Trail of Tears want to experience and remember some of the hardships of 1838.

—Archie Mouse of Tahlequah, Oklahoma,
leader of the 1988 Trail of Tears Wagon Train

In the 1930s, as the hundredth anniversary of the Trail of Tears approached, many newspapers reviewed the tragic story of the Cherokee removal. Historians and reporters collected stories told by descendants of the Cherokees who made the long journey west. Descendants of white pioneers who witnessed the march also had stories to tell.

An Illinois man, John G. Mulcaster, spent nearly two years tracing the trail "from the native land of the Cherokee in western North Carolina," through Tennessee, Kentucky, Illinois, Missouri, Arkansas, and northeast Oklahoma. There had been many changes in the hundred years since 1838, but Mulcaster believed he had located the entire route, "the camps, springs, fords of the principal streams, the crossings of the larger rivers." In talking to Cherokees in both the East and the West, he found feelings of great sadness. "This endless exile is so real . . . that it will ever be remembered as a great wrong."

In the 1950s in Farmington, Missouri, the Council of Garden Clubs established Cherokee Roadside Park to commemorate the journey of the Cannon detachment in 1837. The St. Joseph

Campsite at Rock Creek, St. Francois County, on Missouri Route OO south of Farmington. Cherokee Roadside Park was established in 1952 by the Farmington Council of Garden Clubs and the Missouri Highway Commission to commemorate the Cherokee detachment led by B. B. Cannon. (photograph by A. E. Schroeder)

Lead Mining Company donated land for the park on Little Rock Creek just north of the Madison County–St. Francois County line. The site was located south of Farmington on what was then U.S. Route 61. When a new U.S. Route 61 was built, the commemorative monument was moved to Long Park in Farmington. The roadside area is now fenced in, but travelers can still see the quiet, wooded area on Missouri Route OO, thirteen miles south of Farmington, where Cherokees may have camped during the winters of 1837 and 1838–1839.

In 1956 residents of Cape Girardeau County in southeast Missouri voted a bond issue of $150,000 to buy 3,306 acres of land in the area where many of the Cherokees crossed the Mississippi River and camped. Located ten miles north of Cape Girardeau, between Moccasin Springs and Indian Creek, the

Brother Mark Elder's mural Charity along the Trail of Tears, *at the Visitor Center at the Trail of Tears State Park in Cape Girardeau County. (courtesy Brother Mark Elder)*

Trail of Tears State Park is the only state park in Missouri directly on the Mississippi River. It seems ideal as a commemoration for the Cherokees on the Trail of Tears.

One area of three hundred acres, the Vancil Hollow Natural Area along the Mississippi, resembles the Cherokee ancestral homeland in the East. The trees are more typical of the Appalachian Mountains than of the Ozarks: American beech, tulip poplar, and cucumber magnolia grow there, and the ground of the park is covered with ferns and wildflowers. The Indian Creek Wild Area of the park is covered with hardwood forests of white oak, black oak, sweet gum, and willow, with wild grapevines in the lowlands. Wildlife has been undisturbed for many years.

The land was presented to the state of Missouri by Cape Girardeau County for the purpose of establishing a park to commemorate the Cherokees who died on the trail. The Trail of Tears State Park now has a Visitor and Interpretive Center with museum displays relating to Cherokee history and the

Trail of Tears, a video program, artifacts, and books. A mural by Brother Mark Elder commemorates some of the experiences of the Cherokees who camped at Moccasin Springs in the winter of 1838–1839.

Farther west, the Missouri Department of Conservation has established the White River Trace Wildlife Area in Dent County. One of the routes taken by the Cherokees on the Trail of Tears followed part of the White River Trace. The White River Trace was an ancient Indian trail between St. Louis and Springfield. The Missouri Department of Conservation is restoring native grasses and other vegetation and encouraging increases of all wildlife native to the area. The department plans to highlight the trace as a vital part of the area's history.

To commemorate the 150th anniversary of the Cherokee removal, the U.S. Congress acted to make the Trail of Tears part of the National Historic Trails system. The Trail of Tears National Historic Trail was established in 1987. Over two thousand miles of land and water routes were included in the planned historic trail.

Maps of the corridors were published in 1992 as a supplement to the *Comprehensive Management and Use Plan*, developed by the United States Department of the Interior. The National Park Service has worked with local and state groups to identify and mark the routes. A spokesman for the National Park Service reports that "one of the most visible parts of the program is the auto tour route. Major highways that closely parallel the main overland route are being marked with . . . signs that include the Trail logo." These signs have been installed in Missouri by the Missouri Highway Department. Future plans include programs, exhibits, and publications to tell the story of the Trail of Tears.

The interpretive theme for the Trail of Tears programs planned will relate broadly to the evolution of the U.S. government's Indian removal policy and to the effect this policy had on the Cherokees, according to National Park Service historians. "It is also intended to commemorate the similar experiences of the other four of the Five Civilized Tribes (the

Trail of Tears logo. (courtesy United States Department of the Interior, National Park Service)

Chickasaw, Choctow, Creek, and Seminole tribes) as well as other eastern tribes."

One of the primary aims of the National Park Service is to protect resources along the trail. According to a park service spokesman, "Trail sites that are not on Federal land can only become a part of the Trail of Tears National Historic Trail if the owner or managing authority requests that the site or segment be certified as part of the Trail." Guidelines will be provided for management and protection of the trail's cultural resources, particularly Indian burial grounds and sacred objects. The National Park Service plan calls for immediate notification of the Cherokee tribe if human remains are found.

In 1988 and 1989 there were many individual and group efforts to commemorate the 1838–1839 march. Towns put up markers or planned reenactments. Local historians researched sites relating to the trail in their areas. Markers were placed to enable travelers to find sites of significant events, and known burial grounds were marked.

A group in Madison County organized a fifteen-wagon train to travel from Marquand to Fredericktown, where a three-day

A wagon train retracing the Trail of Tears traveled from Tennessee to Oklahoma in 1988. The wagon representing Missouri stopped in Anna, Illinois, on a cold day in October 1988. (photograph by Mark Sterkel, Southeast Missourian, *October 23, 1988)*

gathering was held. Missourians also saw a larger train, thirty wagons of Cherokees and their friends—members of other tribes and whites—that started where the 1838 trek began and went to Tahlequah, Oklahoma. Along the way people were able to join in and travel along as far as they wished. An average of 120 were marching on any given day, according to Archie Mouse of Tahlequah.

Mouse had been chosen by the tribe to lead the train, and he rode horseback the whole distance. He said, "I wanted to experience a small fraction of the discomfort my ancestors felt, open to the elements, rain or shine. But there were differences. I had a poncho to put on, warm clothes, plenty of food, and a tent at night."

The marchers were asked to speak in classrooms, at civic and social meetings, or sometimes just from the courthouse steps. Mouse was grateful for this opportunity because, he says, "Too many people have no idea what the Trail of Tears was."

Another major event of 1989 was a joint council meeting, with ceremonies and banquets held by the two main branches of the Cherokee tribe. People from Tahlequah invited Cherokees from the Cherokee, North Carolina, area and from elsewhere in the United States. They held a parade to open the two-day Cherokee Fall Festival.

Earlier the tribe had debated whether the anniversary should be observed at all. Many felt it was best forgotten, but others insisted it is necessary to remember. Most agreed with officers of the Trail of Tears Commission that their purpose should be to educate people "so that never again will anything like this happen."

John Hicks, vice principal chief, said, "We need to remember so people will learn from mistakes," and Mike Abrams spoke for many non-Indians participating in the big wagon train when he said, "We can't help what our ancestors did, but we can help what we do."

States in which the Cherokees lived and those along the routes of the many trails taken during the Cherokee removal are restoring buildings and marking sites associated with Cherokee history. The National Park Service *Comprehensive Management and Use Plan* lists many of the historic locations and gives preliminary information about them.

The Trail of Tears Association was created in 1993 and incorporated in Missouri as a nonprofit organization. The corporation papers were signed by both Wilma Mankiller, then principal chief of the Cherokee Nation of Oklahoma, and Jonathan L. Taylor, principal chief of the Eastern Band of Cherokee Indians. The association members work with the National Park Service to promote, protect, and preserve the resources and legacy of the Trail of Tears National Historic Trail.

Missouri Sites on the Trail of Tears

Green's Ferry site at Moccasin Springs in Cape Girardeau County. Here a ferry crossed the Mississippi River from Willard Landing on the Illinois side of the river. This site is ten miles north of Cape Girardeau, near the southern end of what is now the Trail of Tears State Park. Cherokees took the Green's Ferry Road toward Jackson. The ferry site and part of the road are included in the park.

"Otahki" Bushyhead Hildebrand's grave is within the Trail of Tears State Park. A prominent marker commemorates the death of the young woman who symbolizes for many the suffering of the Indians on the Trail.

Snelson-Brinker House in Crawford County. This is a restored log house built in 1834. It is on Missouri Route 8, near what is now the Maramec Iron Works. The Cherokees camped and bought corn here.

Massey (now Maramec) Iron Works in Crawford County, on Missouri Route 8 between Steelville and St. James. The oldest ironworks in the state, the site has stone structures dating from 1829. Dr. Morrow and others wrote of the ironworks. This area is under the management of the James Foundation.

Danforth Farm in Greene County. The Danforth Farm is on Pearson Creek near Missouri Route 125, northeast of Springfield. The Danforth family still owns the property, which was settled by Josiah Danforth in the early 1830s.

Bell Tavern in Greene County. This site is between the James River and Wilson's Creek, south of Springfield in an area where Delaware villages and a Delaware trading post once stood. Here the White River Trace forked to the southeast, while the Cherokees followed the Indian Trace southwest through Stone and Barry Counties.

McMurty Spring in Barry County. This spring is alongside Missouri Route 37, a little over two miles southwest of Cassville. Its water was used by Cherokee groups traveling along Flat Creek.

Note: These are the sites listed in the United States Department of Interior National Park Service *Comprehensive Management and Use Plan: Trail of Tears National Historic Trail,* published in 1992. Since 1992, Bushyhead family research has shown that "Otahki" was Nancy Bushyhead Walker Hildebrand, the sister of Reverend Jesse Bushyhead.

For More Reading

After the Trail of Tears, by William G. McLoughlin (Chapel Hill: University of North Carolina Press, 1993), tells how the Cherokees built up their new homeland despite devastations brought on by the Civil War. It takes their history through 1880.

America's First Big Parade, by an "unknown author," but attributed to Dave Thornton (Little Rock, Ark.: Central Print, 1932), is a fictionalized account of the exile that is interesting to read because of the style of writing. It appears to borrow heavily from the work of James Mooney, an ethnologist who lived with the Cherokees for several years, and uses much material obtained from interviews with people who had walked the Trail of Tears.

The Cherokee Nation of Indians, by Charles C. Royce (Chicago: Aldine Publishing, 1975), is a Smithsonian Institution Press book in the Native American Library series. The series was established to publish original works by Indians and reprints selected by the tribes involved. Royce's report, which was originally published in the *Fifth Annual Report of the Bureau of American Ethnology*, was republished at the request of the Governing Body of the Cherokee Nation. It discusses and provides a historical background and texts of treaties between the United States and the Cherokees from 1785 to 1868. Although it focuses primarily on places and things, it documents an important aspect of Cherokee history.

The Cherokees, by Grace Steele Woodward (Norman: University of Oklahoma Press, 1963), is a volume in the Civilization of the American Indian series and gives a full and detailed history of the Cherokee people.

Cherokee Sunset, a Nation Betrayed, by Samuel Carter III (Garden City, N.Y.: Doubleday, 1976), is a thorough account of the history of the Cherokee people and the Trail of Tears. It presents data primarily from the viewpoint of John Ross.

Cherokee Tragedy: The Ridge Family and the Decimation of a People, by Thurman Wilkins (Norman: University of Oklahoma Press, 1992), tells the story of removal and its aftermath from the Ridge family viewpoint. It is interesting to read this after *Cherokee Sunset, a Nation Betrayed.*

Comprehensive Management and Use Plan: Trail of Tears National Historic Trail (Denver: Denver Service Center, United States Department of Interior, National Park Service, 1992), provides a history of the Trail of Tears and gives information on plans for development of programs for the Trail of Tears National Historic Trail. The map supplement gives details of both the land and the water routes.

Historical Sketch of the Cherokees, by James Mooney (Chicago: Aldine Publishing, 1975), is a Smithsonian Institution Press book in the Native American Library series. This historical sketch was originally published in the *Nineteenth Annual Report of the Bureau of American Ethnology.* Mooney lived with and studied the Cherokees at various times between 1887 and 1890, and his book focuses on people as well as events. His knowledge is based on personal interviews with many members of the tribe, and the book examines many interesting aspects of the Cherokees' traditional culture.

Indian Removal, by Grant Foreman (Norman: University of Oklahoma Press, 1989), is one of the most respected works of its kind, written by an attorney who worked in Oklahoma in the first half of the twentieth century. He knew people who had walked the trail or those whose parents had. He made extensive use of writings of individuals and of gov-

ernment documents pertaining to the removal of the Five
Civilized Tribes.

No Resting Place, by William Humphrey (New York: Delacorte,
1989), is a novel that describes a young Cherokee boy who
learns to take burdensome responsibility on the Trail of
Tears.

Sequoyah: The Cherokee Genius, by Stan Hoig (Oklahoma City:
Oklahoma Historical Society, 1995), is the life story of the
inventor of the Cherokee syllabary and is told against the
backdrop of Cherokee history. Sequoyah's invention made
it possible to write and print the native language of the
Cherokees. The author discusses the many events in Sequoyah's life from his birth in Alabama to his death in
Mexico. His service with General Jackson in the Creek
War, his travels west to Arkansas and Oklahoma, his trips
to Washington on behalf of his people, and his last journey to Mexico are described.

Walk in My Soul, by Lucia St. Clair Robson (New York: Ballan-
tine, 1985), is a novel based on the supposed love affair
between Sam Houston and Tiana Rogers, a Cherokee
woman.

Winds of Destiny, by Laurel Pace (New York: Harlequin Historical, 1994), is a novel that uses very sound research on
what it would have been like to be a Cherokee while the
tribe was being pressured to move.

For More Information

Materials can be obtained from several museums and agencies:

Cherokee National Museum
P.O. Box 515
Tahlequah, OK 74465

Museum of the Cherokee Indian
P.O. Box 1599
Cherokee, NC 28719

Trail of Tears Association
1100 N. University, Suite 133
Little Rock, AR 72207-6344
(501) 666-9032

Trail of Tears Commission, Inc.
P.O. Box 4027
Hopkinsville, KY 42240

Trail of Tears State Park
Missouri Department of Natural Resources
P.O. Box 176
Jefferson City, MO 65102

Index

76–77, 78; supplies on, 2, 29, 34, 35, 38, 42, 51–52, 53, 77; exploitation of Cherokees on, 2, 40, 41–42; kindness toward Cherokees on, 2–3, 45, 50–51, 59, 75; accidents on, 28, 73; origin of name of, 30; soldiers' treatment of Cherokees on, 32–33, 34, 39; protests by onlookers about, 34; animals on, 34, 36, 37, 38, 40, 42, 53, 78; suggestions for water route, 36, 62–63; in Tennessee, 37–43; possessions of Cherokees on, 38, 41, 42, 53, 78; hunting on, 38, 68, 69–70; reenactment of, 106–7; river crossings on, 40–41, 48, 52–53, 54–55, 56, 59; road conditions on, 41; in Kentucky, 44–48; weather conditions on, 45, 47, 50, 53, 57, 61, 64, 65, 66–67, 68, 72, 77; in Illinois, 48–55; camp life on, 49–50, 68–69; in Missouri, 55, 56–75; young people's games on, 68; in Arkansas, 76–79; clothing of Cherokees on, 78; 100th anniversary of, 102; 150th anniversary of, 105, 106–8. *See also* Deaths on Trail of Tears; Illness on Trail of Tears; Stockades
Trail of Tears group leaders, 37, 42. *See also* Bell, John A.; Benge, John; Bushyhead, Jesse; Cannon, B. B.; Foreman, Stephen; Hicks, Elijah; Hildebrand, Peter; Jones, Evan; Powell, J.; Taylor, Richard; Young, John S.
Trail of Tears National Historic Trail, 105, 106, 108
Trail of Tears State Park, 57, 59, 104–5, 109
Treaty of New Echota. *See* New Echota, Treaty of
Treaty of 1791, 5–6, 14
Treaty of 1817, 18
Treaty of 1828, 20
Treaty Party: one of two factions in tribe before emigration, 20; signs Treaty of New Echota, 21–22; seizes *Cherokee Phoenix*, 24; six hundred members of, emigrate west, 25, 28; group of, refuses to travel with Ross followers, 57; resentment toward, 80; deaths of three leaders

of, 81–84; adopts a resolution against Ross, 85; members of, emigrate to Texas, 86
Tyler, John, 85

Union County, Ill., 50
United States: government mistakes in planning Cherokee removal, 1–2; government promises to Cherokees, 2, 6, 15–16, 20, 32, 35–36, 41, 43, 79–80, 86; Congress, 2, 11, 13, 105; government officials and John Ross, 9; Constitution, 12; Supreme Court, 14; government pushes for Cherokee removal, 15; Senate, 22–23, 25; members of government of, oppose forced removal, 23; no help from government of, for Georgia abuses, 25; government provisions for removal, 39; House of Representatives, 85; government recognizes Cherokees in the West, 99

Van Buren, Martin: elected president, 15; letter to, from Ralph Waldo Emerson, 23; refuses to grant delay on removal, 25; reports to Congress on removal, 44–45; turns down Cherokee claims for additional funds, 80; refuses to recognize Ross as chief, 85

Walini, 73, 79
Washburn, Mo., 75
Washington, George, 5
Washington County, Ark., 77
Washington County, Mo., 61, 75
Watie, Stand, 83, 86, 88
Waynesville, Mo., 62, 75
Webster, Daniel, 12
Webster County, Mo., 75
White Path, 40, 45
White River, 62, 74
White River Trace, 70–71, 105
White Rock Creek, 81
Willard Landing, Ill., 57
Wool, Gen. Ellis, 27, 31–32
Worcester, Samuel, 14, 83, 88

Young, John S., 28

About the Author

Joan Gilbert is a full-time writer who lives near Hallsville with several pets and many books and trees. She has published two novels and hundreds of pieces of short fiction and nonfiction, winning first-place awards from the National Federation of Press Women, the Missouri Press Women, the Missouri Writers Guild, the Ozarks Writers League, and the James-Younger Gang. She is a native Missourian and a graduate of Southwest Missouri State College in Springfield. She was a public-relations and newspaper writer before becoming a freelance writer.